PARENTS WHO CHEAT

PARENTS who CHEAT

How Children and Adults Are Affected When Their Parents Are Unfaithful

Ana Nogales, Ph.D.

with Laura Golden Bellotti

Health Communications, Inc.
Deerfield Beach, Florida

www.hcibooks.com

Library of Congress Cataloging-in-Publication Data

Nogales, Ana, 1951-
  Parents who cheat : how children and adults are affected when their parents are unfaithful / Ana Nogales with Laura Golden Bellotti.
    p. cm.
  Includes bibliographical references.
  ISBN-13: 978-0-7573-0652-5
  ISBN-10: 0-7573-0652-7
  1. Adultery—Psychological aspects.   2. Parents—Family relationships.
  I. Bellotti, Laura Golden.   II. Title.
  HQ806.N64 2009
  306.73'6—dc22

                                                                    2009012227

Publisher: Health Communications, Inc.
        3201 S.W. 15th Street
        Deerfield Beach, FL 33442–8190

Cover design by Larissa Hise Henoch
Interior design and formatting by Lawna Patterson Oldfield

All my best
in your journey!

D. De hofer

8-19-05

To my family,
from whom I learned
about love and loyalty

"Forgiveness is the final form of love."

—Reinhold Niebuhr

CONTENTS

ACKNOWLEDGMENTS

I am deeply grateful to my literary agent, Susan Schulman, for her warm support and strong belief in this book.

I extend many thanks to our editor, Michele Matrisciani, for her enthusiasm and wise editorial guidance.

I would also like to thank Dr. Sonnee Weedn, who was instrumental in helping to access the resources and networks to launch our Parents Who Cheat Survey.

I appreciate, as well, the generous efforts of Dr. Nora Comstock, who helped us spread the word about the Parents Who Cheat Survey.

I am forever grateful to Yolanda Hernandez, my right hand, who is always there to facilitate my work. With her assistance I am able to do so much more.

And, finally, my heartfelt gratitude to the women and men who openly and graciously shared their experiences of dealing with a parent's infidelity.

INTRODUCTION

Over the thirty-three years of my clinical practice, I have heard from hundreds of clients about the painful repercussions in a child's life when one parent betrays the other. I felt compelled to write this book because I believe the effects of parental infidelity on children of all ages is a profoundly important issue that has been largely ignored. While much has been written about the impact of divorce on children, and although there are numerous books on how couples can cope with the fallout of marital infidelity, little attention has been paid to how children are affected by a parent's unfaithfulness. What are the emotional consequences for the child—young or adult—when his or her parent cheats? How can parents undergoing an infidelity crisis help their child cope with his or her reactions? And how might adult children deal with their own parental infidelity-related issues? My objective was to write a comprehensive book for mainstream readers that would address these overarching questions.

Young children, as well as teens and young adults, may respond to their parent's infidelity with shock, confusion, rage, cynicism, sadness, shame, or a combination of these reactions. While they have nothing to do with one parent's decision to cheat on the other, children are often left feeling guilty, hopeless, tainted, or damaged—words they often use. As adults, children whose parents cheated are frequently unable to enjoy a healthy relationship because they are plagued by a profound lack of trust, an attraction to partners who cheat, or a proclivity toward infidelity themselves.

Once I knew I wanted to write this book, part of my research involved undertaking a survey of adult *children of infidelity*. I've created the term *children of infidelity* to identify children of any age whose parent or parents engaged in one or more extramarital affairs.[1] I wanted to find out more about how children are affected when one or both parents cheat. Seventy-five percent of those who responded to our "Parents Who Cheat" survey reported that they felt betrayed by the parent who cheated. Sixty-two percent felt ashamed. Eighty percent felt that their attitude toward love and relationships was influenced by their parent having cheated, and 70 percent said that their ability to trust others had been affected. Eighty-three percent stated that they feel people regularly lie. And yet, 86 percent reported that they still believe in monogamy! The complete survey results can be found in the Appendix, but beyond the percentages, the stories these adult children of infidelity tell about how their lives were impacted by a parent's unfaithfulness reveal a more complete and poignant picture. You'll hear many of these compelling stories throughout the book.

Some people may contend that my book is based on an outdated premise; namely, that parental monogamy is healthier for children than parental infidelity. Infidelity is so common, some may argue, and even justified in many cases, that children these days can easily adapt. I'll admit that there are a number of seemingly reasonable justifications for marital infidelity. Some claim that because people live longer nowadays, it is unrealistic to expect married couples to be faithful throughout their lives. Others point to the fact that modern life means women and men engage in more varied experiences outside the home and have greater opportunities to interact with new people, thus making sexual affairs more inevitable. And there are those who argue that our culture's liberalized sexual mores have made marital fidelity anachronistic.

In spite of those who believe that monogamy is a thing of the past, research proves otherwise. A 2008 Gallup poll on moral issues found that 91 percent believed married men or women having an affair is morally wrong. My survey indicates that children still expect fidelity and loyalty between their parents, and adult children whose parents cheated still want monogamous relationships themselves. By and large, adult children of infidelity know from experience the extent to which the whole family suffers when a parent is unfaithful, and therefore most do not want to follow in their unfaithful parents' footsteps.

I believe that it is within the spirit of humankind to create, nurture, and sustain healthy, monogamous relationships from which both couples and children benefit. Even in our modern age, most men and women continue to seek a lifelong partner, and couples who marry continue to promise and expect sexual fidelity. When they do, their future children are rooted in that promise. Sexual affairs break the promise through secrecy and lies, and children can't help but feel the painful effects, regardless of their age. According to the survey undertaken for this book, as well as the hundreds of clients I have treated, most children are hurt by their parent's infidelity because, like the deceived parent, they feel betrayed. And like 93 percent of the American public,[2] they still believe that marital fidelity is the most important element in a successful marriage.

ONE

When Parents Break Their Promise

I think it made me very afraid of intimacy for many, many years. It did color every relationship I had with women. I'm not sure if I trusted women, for a long, long time.[3]

—*Sting, referring to his mother's affair, which he discovered when he was a young boy*

The pledge to be faithful to one's spouse is our culture's most highly regarded vow. When parents break it, they also break an unspoken promise to their children: to be part of a loving family whose members are forever loyal to each other. Although the effect of marital infidelity on children is an explosive subject that touches millions of homes across America, it is rarely considered or discussed. But whether a child is six, sixteen, or twenty-six, when his parents sexually betray each other, he is left with a host of psychological issues that can plague him for the rest of his life.

As permissive as our society has become since the sexual revolution of the 1960s and 1970s, children still expect their parents to love each other and treat each other honorably. Infidelity may be the stuff of numerous movies and TV dramas, but most kids want to believe that "it can't happen here." Unfortunately, it does, and finding out that one of your parents has cheated on the other is a crushing emotional blow. How does such a betrayal alter a child's relationship to the unfaithful parent—and to the betrayed mother or father? Will a young child's ability to trust his parents be undermined? Will an older child ever be able to trust a romantic partner? Are adult children of infidelity, supposedly wiser to the ways of the world, any less troubled by a parent's unfaithfulness than their younger counterparts? These are some of the core questions we will be exploring together.

Whatever their age, children whose parents have been unfaithful are often pressured to become the caretaker of the betrayed parent, thus adding to the son's or daughter's emotional stress. Young children may be unable to articulate their anger, anxiety, and confusion. They might act out, regress, or withdraw. And when an adult child's family baggage includes lies, cheating, and the breaking of promises, they may have a particularly hard time navigating the rough waters of dating and marriage. The bottom line is that when parents are role models of infidelity, their children can't help but react. We'll be examining the range of those emotional and behavioral responses— and how to deal with them—throughout this book. In the chapters to come, I will suggest ways that parents can minimize the negative effects of infidelity on a child, and I will offer adult children advice for dealing with problems that may have originated with a parent's unfaithfulness.

In this chapter, I want to give you an overview of what children experience when their parents are unfaithful, so I'll be introducing the six core responses to parental infidelity.[4] I'll also offer my thoughts on how parental infidelity impacts the stages in a child's social and emotional development, as presented by prominent psychiatrist Erik Erikson. Whether you are the betrayed or the unfaithful spouse, I will help you understand what your child is going through emotionally. If you are an adult child of an unfaithful parent (or parents), you'll begin to gain a deeper insight into how your parent's infidelity has impacted your life and your relationships. We'll also take a look at the relevant statistics on infidelity, attitudes surrounding it, and how parental infidelity figures into our cultural environment. And you'll hear the stories of four children, ranging in age from six to forty, whose lives were deeply affected when one parent was unfaithful to the other.

Millions of adults and children are grappling with the emotional crises that parental infidelity ushers in. Learning about how some of these individuals have worked through their infidelity-related issues will encourage you to take steps to meaningfully deal with yours. In the following chapters, I'll offer guidance concerning those important steps. But first, let's explore the problem.

A COMMON FAMILY DRAMA

Statistics regarding the percentage of spouses who engage in extramarital affairs vary considerably. According to psychiatrist Scott Haltzman, whose research is cited in the July 26, 2004, issue of *Psychology Today,* infidelity occurs in up to 40 percent of marriages. Dr. Haltzman asserts that by age forty-five, two out of every five men and one out of every five women has had at least one affair. In a survey conducted in 2007 by MSNBC.com and iVillage, 19 percent of male survey respondents and 12 percent of female survey respondents reported having sexual intercourse with someone other than their partner; of those women, 37 percent cheated while there was a child in the home.

If we include cybersex, which can involve self-stimulation with an online partner, there are even more instances of infidelity. Although there is no indication of how many respondents were married, an online survey of 38,000 Internet users found that one in ten reported being addicted to online sex. Twenty-five percent stated they had lost control of their Internet sexual exploits at least once or that the activity caused problems in their lives.[5] Some married individuals who engage in cybersex don't consider their activities as being unfaithful to their spouse. Only 46 percent of the men queried in one study believe that online affairs are adultery.[6]

Most of us still believe in fidelity in marriage, regardless of the small percentage who think it is an outdated concept. In a 2000 study of college students' attitudes toward infidelity, 69 percent said they would end a relationship with a partner who was unfaithful.[7] And a 2007 survey by the Pew Research Center found that 93 percent of respondents rated faithfulness as the most important component of a successful marriage—more important than a happy sexual relationship, shared interests, religious beliefs, adequate income, or having children.

Still, infidelity is a fact of life in both the real and virtual worlds, and it often makes the headlines when powerful people are involved. President Bill Clinton's affair with a young intern nearly brought the government to a halt, but he is not alone among politicians who have cheated on their wives. More recently, incidents of adultery came to light involving a 2008 presidential candidate as well as the governor of New York and the mayors of both San Francisco and Los Angeles. When it was revealed that the mayor of Los Angeles was having an extramarital relationship with a television anchorwoman, his constituents weighed in on the significance of his behavior. Many of the letters to the editor in the *Los Angeles Times* posed this rhetorical question: If he lies and cheats on his wife, how do we know he doesn't lie and cheat in his role as mayor? There was also reference to the mayor's alleged hypocrisy, since he had presented an image of a family man who cared deeply about the welfare of families—which brings up the point most relevant to this book. With all the attention paid to high-profile cases of infidelity involving politicians and others in the public eye, there is rarely any discussion of how acts of sexual betrayal affect the betrayer's children. And yet I have had a number of clients, themselves children of parents who cheated, tell me that uppermost in their minds when the governor's or the mayor's infidelities were revealed was how the children of these well-known men must have felt. "I was so humiliated when my father cheated on my mother, I could really feel for what the governor's three teenage daughters were going through," one client told me recently.

How does a teenager who adores both her father and her mother get on with her life when that young life has been temporarily shattered by her father's lies and humiliating indiscretions? How does a young boy make sense of what Daddy did with another woman, something that made Mommy want to separate from him? These are the questions that are too often ignored, both in the public arena and in the fictional dramas that are part of our cultural environment.

UNFAITHFUL ON THE SCREEN

The infidelity we may have experienced or witnessed in real life is often mirrored in our popular culture. From opera to blues and country songs, serious dramas to *Desperate Housewives*, cheating frequently gets star billing. What is rarely featured is adultery's effect on the cheater's son or daughter. One of the first—and only—films to show how a child is affected by his parent's unfaithfulness was the 1944 Vittorio De Sica classic, *The Children Are Watching Us*, in which a four-year-old boy witnesses his mother meeting her lover in the park and later lying with him on the beach. While in the first instance the couple is merely standing opposite each other and having a conversation, the boy intuits from their expressions and body language that they are intimately connected. In an instant, his face loses its carefree innocence and conveys shock, fear, and rage. Later in the film when the boy comes upon his mother and the man lying together in the sand, an extreme close-up of the child's face reveals overwhelming anguish, as if his entire world is crumbling before his eyes. When discussing the film, De Sica is said to have remarked that, "Children are the first to suffer in life. . . . Innocents always pay."[8]

Although societal mores have changed over the last sixty-plus years since this film was first released, the pain a child feels when one of his parents betrays the other continues to be just as devastating. Twenty-eight percent of the respondents to my survey were under the age of eleven when they discovered a parent was cheating. In almost every case I have come across, young children report feeling as if they have been betrayed when one parent betrays the other. The child identifies with the parent who has been betrayed because he is suffering immeasurable loss as well—the loss of trust in one or both parents, the loss of both parents' ability to be an attentive parent, the loss of faith in the cohesiveness of the family, and, of course, a loss of innocence.

If the betrayed parent holds back his or her emotions, as was the case with the betrayed father in *The Children Are Watching Us*, the child often acts out the parent's anguish and resentment in addition to expressing his own. Many parents, perhaps fathers especially, try to appear "strong" so as not to communicate their pain to the child and thus exacerbate the young person's anger and sadness. But children cannot be fooled so easily. They pick up on their parents' emotions even when a parent is attempting to keep those feelings in check. And children are also more apt to express their emotions directly, as the child in the De Sica film so achingly displays.

The essential truth that De Sica masterfully brings home to his audience in this film is that children are betrayed when one or both parents cheat. While the betrayed parent, like the film's father, may not expect anything from the betraying spouse once infidelity has been discovered, a child is still left with hopeful expectations, as well as a host of fears. A child of infidelity finds himself caught in a nightmare that offers few viable options: either accept the unacceptable—namely, being betrayed by your parent, who is supposed to give you unconditional love—and hope that doing so will ensure your parent's love and attention, or express your outrage and risk being abandoned by the person whose love you so desperately want and need.

While not always portrayed as sensitively as in *The Children Are Watching Us*, extramarital affairs continue to figure into the plotlines of countless television and film scenarios. After all, cheating on a spouse makes for an intriguing, suspenseful, sexy story. Will the husband find out? Will the wife feel remorse? Will she run away with her lover and begin a more passionate, romantic life? While we might enjoy watching such dramas unfold, their popularity doesn't mean that the average TV viewer or filmgoer approves of a character's marital infidelity, especially when the cheating spouse is a parent. According to a recent *Wall Street Journal* editorial by author Lionel Shriver, screenwriters are keenly aware of the audience's general disapproval of philanderers. Shriver asserts that for audiences to sympathize with a character who indulges in extramarital sex, the betrayed spouse needs to have a major flaw. For instance, in the film

Little Children, starring Kate Winslet as the unfaithful housewife and mother drawn to a handsome, sensitive lover, her husband is portrayed as an unappealing weirdo who is addicted to Internet pornography. And yet, as in other film and television stories featuring unfaithful spouses, the housewife's affair is ultimately abandoned for the sake of the children—hers as well as her lover's. In the end, Winslet's character cannot bring herself to sacrifice her family for the sake of her passionate yearnings. Thus, claims Shriver, "The audience is relieved."[9]

Extramarital sex is both a fact of life and a familiar tale featured on the big and little screens, but regardless of how common infidelity appears to be or how thrilling a love story it may present, when it occurs within one's own family, it is never easy for children of any age to understand or accept. As much as we might think that sexual mores have changed radically since the more repressed 1950s, some expectations haven't changed. Most children still want and expect their parents to be a faithful couple. Children are more likely to thrive when their parents are stable and focused on the family rather than on an outside romantic relationship. In other words, kids seem to be hardwired to prefer that their parents resemble characters like Ozzie and Harriet, rather than Kate Winslet and her handsome lover.

THE SIX CORE RESPONSES TO PARENTAL INFIDELITY

Every family is different, each child is unique, and yet there are certain common responses to parental infidelity that most children experience. The 822 respondents to the survey that I conducted for this book, as well as the many clients I have treated over the years, have confirmed that the following are core responses experienced by offspring of every age—from young children to adults—after they find out that one or both of their parents have been sexually unfaithful:

1. **Loss of trust** (including fear of rejection and abandonment and loss of self-esteem). A loving relationship is supposed to mean that both people can be counted on to have the other's best interests at heart. Even young children understand that marriage is supposed to involve taking care of each other, being kind to each other, and not lying to or intentionally hurting your husband or wife. Infidelity brings about just the opposite: fights, anger, sadness, and pain—along with concrete evidence of a fundamental lie. When children of any age learn of a parent's infidelity, they usually find it extremely difficult—if not impossible—to trust that someone they love will not lie to them, reject or abandon them, or otherwise cause them pain somewhere down the road. They very often learn not to put their faith in love, and they may also learn that they are not worthy of receiving monogamous love, because according to the evidence, their betrayed parent clearly wasn't.

2. **Shame** (for being part of a family in which at least one parent has betrayed life's most valued commitment). Even though the child of an unfaithful parent is blameless, very often he or she cannot help but feel ashamed, as if the entire family is under the dark cloud of the transgressor's offensive behavior. Relatives, friends, or neighbors may ask embarrassing questions about the details of a parent's infidelity, inadvertently exacerbating a son's or daughter's belief that the shameful behavior somehow reflects on their own character. It is as if the betraying parent's sexual transgression becomes a black mark against the child and the rest of the immediate family. The sense of

shame about his parent's affair(s) is often carried forward into the adult child's own relationships.

3. **Confusion** (about the meaning of love and marriage). Most children are taught that when you love someone enough to marry them, it means you vow to be faithful to that person. When marriage includes infidelity, what conclusions do children draw? That marriage is a sham? That married love is an illusion? Fifty-eight percent of our respondents stated that their parents stayed married even when the betraying parent continued having affairs and the betrayed parent knew about the infidelity. The effect on the children in such relationships was profound confusion about the meaning of both love and marriage.

4. **Ambivalence toward the betraying parent** (feeling anger and disrespect, but also needing to love and respect one's mother or father). Children initially look up to their parents as the most important people in their lives, their ultimate role models, and, in some sense, their heroes. As children grow older, they want to continue to be proud of who their parents are. When infidelity partially defines a parent's character, a son or daughter feels torn between feelings of disrespect and a yearning to preserve the revered status their parent once held. Children of unfaithful parents may feel both love and hatred toward the parent who cheated. Some even express this emotional conflict in terms of there being two mothers or two fathers—the one who used to be their parent (and was deserving of their love) and the one who was revealed when the infidelity was brought to light (and whom they now "hate"). Some children are afraid to express their anger for fear of losing the love of the parent who cheated; others report that it took them years to feel anything other than anger toward the betraying parent.

5. **Resentment toward the betrayed parent** (for requiring the child to become their emotional caretaker or for underparenting due to preoccupation with the infidelity drama). In addition to feeling betrayed by the cheating parent, many children feel betrayed as well by the cheated-on parent, who is often unable to adequately fulfill his or her parenting role. The betrayed parent, who may be extremely depressed and angry following the news of a spouse's infidelity, may not only neglect parental responsibilities but also depend on the child to fulfill emotional needs that were previously filled by the spouse. In such cases, the child becomes a surrogate parent and/or surrogate mate to the parent, which is an unhealthy situation for both parent and child. The child longs for an authentic parent and at the same time resents being placed in the unwanted role of caretaker. A child may also resent the betrayed parent for being incapable of preventing the other parent's infidelity. A common accusation is that the cheated-on parent was "too weak" and thus let the cheating parent get away with it.

6. **Acting out** (engaging in aggressive or self-destructive behavior, rather than confronting confusing, sad, or angry feelings directly). Acting out may include behavioral problems during childhood, sexual acting out during adolescence, and intimacy avoidance or sexual addiction during adult years. Issues of promiscuity may arise in an attempt to play out what a child perceived from his parents about the casualness of sex and the impermanence of love and marriage. He may unconsciously try to justify the transgressor parent's behavior or to search for responses to his innermost conflicts concerning whether or not love, loyalty, and commitment are possible.

As you'll learn in the following case histories, when parents are unfaithful, a son's or daughter's responses incorporate one or more of these six core issues, regardless of how old the child is when he or she first learns of the infidelity.

RESPONDING TO PARENTAL INFIDELITY: FOUR STORIES

Brittany's Story: Loss of Trust and Acting Out

Brittany was six when she heard her mother crying hysterically behind her parents' locked bedroom door. When she asked her father what was wrong with Mommy, he told her only that, "Mommy is not feeling well." Still confused about why her mother was so upset, Brittany went to her nine-year-old brother, who told her, "Dad has a girlfriend, and he loves her more than Mom." Overwhelmed by her father's lie and the sense that he didn't love his family anymore, Brittany became angry, sad, and bewildered—and began acting out by throwing temper tantrums.

Brittany's father didn't want to end the marriage to Brittany's mother; he considered the affair merely transitory and had hoped it would be kept secret. When Brittany's mother found out, however, she accused him of not loving her anymore, and she wasn't at all sure she wanted to stay married to him. While the couple was in the midst of sorting out their relationship, the children inadvertently became involved in the infidelity drama. Neither parent had wanted to tell their children about the father's affair, but Brittany's brother had overheard a heated conversation, and Brittany couldn't help but hear her mother sobbing in the bedroom.

Too young at six to understand the nuances of her father's infidelity,

Brittany only knew what she had witnessed (Mommy was terribly unhappy) and what she had been told by her nine-year-old brother (Daddy loved another lady more than he loved Mommy). Brittany was left to conclude that not only did Daddy not love Mommy but he didn't love her or her brother either. She was also left with an overwhelming sense of betrayal, since her father had demonstrated that he could not be trusted to tell her the truth. She was unable to articulate the range of emotions she was feeling—fear, sadness, confusion, anger—but what she could do was act out her anger by having temper tantrums.

Very often adults believe that children will not understand what is happening in the parents' relationship. But while young children may not have the cognitive skills to understand a parent's explanation of a particular situation, they can empirically decipher what is going on. Brittany was able to discern that her father's answer was untrue, and in this instance she trusted her brother more than either of her parents to tell her the truth, because her father's explanation simply didn't ring true. The reason that children often trust other children more than their parents is that they know they can depend on each other to communicate in a simple, straightforward manner.

In an attempt to protect children from the realities of infidelity, many parents either disregard them by failing to offer any explanation at all, minimize the situation by telling a half-truth, or simply lie. Each of these choices then becomes a second betrayal, as children will eventually have to deal with not only their parent's infidelity but having been deceived and/or lied to themselves. In the chapters to come, we'll discover how parents can discuss the issue of infidelity with young children in a way that is both honest and age-appropriate, so that children like Brittany and her brother have an easier time coping with a tough reality.

Michael's Story: Loss of Trust and Living with Shame

Michael was thirteen when he found out that his father had a mistress, but he kept the secret for several weeks to protect his mother. Feeling terribly guilty for betraying her, he finally told his mom, which ultimately resulted in his parents divorcing and Michael believing that he was responsible.

Michael had been placed in an incredibly unfair position. He was forced to choose between being loyal to his father and disloyal to his mother—or vice versa. Whichever choice he made, he felt that he would lose the love and support of one or the other parent. In other words, he couldn't trust either parent to be there for him unconditionally. Sadly, making the decision he made resulted in his bearing the shame and guilt for having brought to light his father's infidelity, as well as feeling that he had caused the dissolution of his parents' marriage. No child should be placed in such a heart-wrenching position. However, many children are taken into the confidence of the betraying parent and told not to tell, while others discover "the secret" on their own and reveal it without even knowing they are doing so. The degree of guilt and shame that results is immeasurable.

Since children are egocentric, feeling that their immediate world revolves around them, they believe that whatever goes wrong is their fault. So when a child experiences a series of events like Michael did—discovering his father's infidelity, telling his mother about it, and then having his parents split up—he is likely to piece the events together in a simple cause-effect fashion: "A crisis came about because I divulged a secret, so everything that happened after that is all my fault." This egocentric way of thinking is often as true for adolescents as it is for younger children. And when a child of any age feels responsible for his parents' breakup, the sense of shame causes a major blow to his self-esteem.

Witnessing his father's disloyalty to his mother, Michael will not only have a problem trusting his father, he may also have problems trusting others to whom he might choose to get close. Michael will always be aware of the fact that the most important man in his life (his father) betrayed his wife (Michael's mother), which will leave Michael with the unfortunate lesson that men cannot be trusted to be faithful to the women they supposedly love the most. And perhaps Michael will distrust anyone who tries to get close to him.

A son or daughter who learns that a parent has cheated becomes particularly angry at such a monumental display of disloyalty, because loyalty is a major issue among school-age children and adolescents. Proving one's loyalty to friends is a crucial endeavor for children and adolescents, since it helps them to gain favor with social groups to which young people feel the need to belong. Belonging is an important part of forming one's identity, and being loyal to the group is always expected of each member. Ashamed of being disloyal to the betraying parent for telling his secret and disloyal to the betrayed parent for being the messenger of bad news, an adolescent like Michael may also find it difficult to trust others for fear they might put him in a similarly unfair bind.

Rebecca's Story: Ambivalence Toward the Betraying Parent and Confusion About the Meaning of Love and Marriage

Rebecca, twenty-eight, was stunned to learn that her mother was cheating on her father. "It's only a fling," her mother told her, "and it has really rejuvenated me. I still love your father and won't ever leave him. Besides, if he doesn't know about it, how can it hurt him?" Although Rebecca considered herself to be a sophisticated young woman, she couldn't believe her mother would do such a thing—and felt as if she had lost her own emotional and moral foundation. She had always admired her mother's outgoing personality and charm and had found her more fun to be with than her rather conservative father. But now she was torn between the mother she thought she knew and the woman who had emerged as someone entirely different.

Girls learn from their mothers how to be a woman, but Rebecca lost her bearings when she felt that she no longer had a suitable role model. She had been taught the importance of being loyal when she was younger, but she now realized it had been merely talk. In fact, her mother was now giving her the opposite message: cheating is okay if it makes you feel better about yourself. Rebecca couldn't help but wonder: if these wildly different messages about love and marriage were so contradictory, then perhaps everything she had learned from her mother—and from her own experiences as well—was equally questionable.

From the time she first learned of her mother's infidelity, Rebecca began questioning everything—her relationships with men, her belief in the family values she had been raised with, even her chosen career path. It was as if everything she had believed in had been crushed under the weight of her mother's shocking behavior. It would take her years before she would discover her own truths and trust in her own choices. In the meantime, she was profoundly disillusioned and disappointed in her mother, confused about what it meant to be a woman, and distrustful of her own romantic choices.

Henry's Story: Ambivalence Toward the Betraying Parent, Resentment Toward the Betrayed Parent, and Acting Out by Engaging in Infidelity Himself

Forty-year-old Henry had been devastated as a child when his parents' marriage fell apart after his father had been unfaithful to his mother one too many times. As a teenager, he had served as his mother's spy, following his father around at night as he visited different women and then reporting back to his mother. When he was twenty-five and about to get married, Henry vowed to his future wife that he would never do what his father had done. Twenty years later, when Henry's wife found out that he had been having affairs for the past ten years, Henry began to ask himself, "How did I fall into the same behavior I so detested in my father?"

Unfortunately, Henry's story is a very common one. For some adult children, even though they disapproved of their parent's unfaithfulness when they were younger, infidelity becomes a more acceptable option when they reach adulthood. Perhaps a parent had provided reasons for his or her unfaithful behavior, and those reasons can be read as a valid "excuse" by the child, who then replicates that behavior as an adult. For other adult children, the parent's infidelity creates a need for emotional distance, and cheating is the best way to create that distance from your partner.

The previous four stories show that children at every age react to the crisis of parental infidelity in a number of predictable ways. In our quest to fully understand how the lives of children and young adults are affected when one parent is unfaithful to the other, it is important to know a little bit about the developmental stages we each go through on our way to adulthood—and how infidelity plays a part in a child's navigation through those stages.

HOW DOES PARENTAL INFIDELITY IMPACT A CHILD'S DEVELOPMENT?

Of the eight developmental stages introduced by psychiatrist Erik Erikson in 1956, the first five especially affect the developing child. These stages give us a fundamental understanding of the process children and teenagers must go through to mature emotionally and socially. When we are familiar with how a child's development unfolds, we can better understand how the crisis of parental infidelity impacts a young person's social and emotional growth.

According to Erikson, each of the eight developmental stages represents a challenge or crisis that an individual must resolve if he is to develop a healthy personality and sense of self. If he fails to complete a particular stage, he will have difficulty in completing further stages. Here are the first five stages that occur between infancy and late adolescence:

- Stage 1 takes place from infancy to age one or two, and it involves learning basic trust. If a child is nurtured and loved, he develops trust and a sense of security; if not, he feels insecure and learns to mistrust that his needs will be met.
- In Stage 2, occurring between about eighteen months to about four years old, the child's task is to gain a certain degree of control so that he becomes more certain of himself and can feel proud of his growing autonomy. If children are made to feel guilty or are neglected or overly criticized, their sense of shame will inhibit their ability to thrive during this stage.
- Stage 3 takes place roughly during the preschool years, when a child usually learns to take initiative, cooperate with others, lead as well as follow, broaden his play skills, and use his imagination. If a child is overly fearful, his play skills and imagination will be inhibited, he won't be able to get along as well with others and will instead be overly dependent on adults.
- The challenges of Stage 4 are typically met during the elementary school years. The key to successfully progressing through this stage is in developing the confidence and self-discipline neces-

sary to be industrious and adapt to rules—those imposed by peers as well as those involved in structured play and in school-work. When a child successfully passes through this developmental stage, he feels increasingly trusting, autonomous, competent, and motivated. When the confidence and self-discipline needed to be successful are not in place due to a sense of shame, guilt, or lack of trust, a child will feel inferior and defeated.

• The process of solidifying one's sense of identity is at the core of Stage 5 of development, which takes place during adolescence. This is a time of experimentation and rebellion in an effort to discover one's values, abilities, preferences, and life goals. A young person successfully passing through this stage experiences some degree of achievement, as opposed to feeling paralyzed by inferiority or inadequacy. He will seek a mentor or role model to inspire him to fulfill his goals. In later adolescence, he or she will also have a clear sense of his or her sexual identity.

So how is this developmental process affected by the crisis of parental infidelity? Let's explore each stage to consider what might occur.

Stage 1

Some claim that very young children don't remember what happens during the first two years of life. But children at this age can perceive whether or not they feel safe with Mom or Dad. If one parent betrays the other, and one or both parents is distressed, angry, sad, or in shock, a one- or two-year-old, even an infant, can sense those emotions and feel very insecure. A betrayed parent might be less attentive toward a baby or young child, or might communicate his or her pain to the youngster directly, believing the child doesn't understand. The betrayer might feel less affection for or give less time to the infant or young child. Either parent might inadvertently take out their anger on the child. The underlying reality is that even very young children pick up on their parents' emotional states, identify with the feeling of being betrayed, and suffer from being neglected. Such circumstances result in a child losing the sense of trust and security that is so crucial at this stage of emotional development.

Stage 2

Even if a young child doesn't understand the intricacies of the infidelity drama, they perceive the general atmosphere in the home and know that something is seriously wrong between Mommy and Daddy. A young child will feel their parents' recriminating attitudes, insecurities, anxiety, and depression, even though they are unable to put a name to it. The crisis environment and sense of uneasiness makes a young child feel unsafe, and thus it will be very difficult for him to emerge from this stage of childhood with a sense of newfound autonomy and pride. Instead, he is likely to feel ashamed that he is not able to be as self-assured as others his age.

Stage 3

When there is upheaval within the family system, it's very difficult for a preschooler to play freely and to be imaginative in play. Often a child whose family is going through a crisis will reenact the traumatic events during play, trying to make sense of or solve whatever conflicts are troubling him. Thus, his imagination is no longer free to explore the world around him during play; the context of his playtime has been dictated by his parents' difficulties. The developmental task of learning cooperation with others may be affected as well, because when there is a problem in the family, every member of that family is implicated. Many children at this age feel that everything that is happening to Mom and Dad is somehow caused by them. Perhaps a child feels that because he had a temper tantrum or misbehaved, Mommy and Daddy are arguing and threatening to split up—so he bears the guilt. Or he may be fearful of being abandoned due to the crisis. While a young child may not understand his parents' recriminating words, he can sense in their tone and body language an impending family catastrophe. As for learning to both lead and follow among his peers—an important developmental milestone—most likely the insecurity and lack of safety that a preschool-age child feels as a consequence of the infidelity drama will make him a follower rather than a leader.

Stage 4

This is a stage when rules are crucial and need to be very clearly set and reaffirmed by parents. Children depend on rules and on structure, but if Mom or Dad is sabotaging the rules, a young person's moral compass goes haywire, and life becomes chaotic. School-age children will likely view the infidelity crisis in terms of rules. They will attempt to assess which rules have been broken to understand what's going on at home. If parents appear to be breaking rules that they themselves had set forth ("it's wrong to lie," "it's wrong to cheat," "family comes first," "being married means loving each other forever"), the child can't help but mistrust both the parent and the rules.

At this stage of development, children are learning how to treat their friends. They're discovering that friendships can also bring pain, due to cheating, gossiping, and making fun of each other. If they have witnessed lying, cheating, and mocking between Mom and Dad, it may be more difficult for them to learn how to deal with others with whom they want to be friends. School-age children know through their own social interactions what it means to be a victim and what it is to be a transgressor, and they can identify with both. When they play, issues of cheating and betrayal often come up. Children are reassured by parents and teachers that cheating is not allowed, that it's not right, that it's not respectful of others, and that it hurts other people. When Mom or Dad or both parents cheat in their relationship, a child at this developmental stage may ask themselves whether or not cheating is really wrong. Is hurting other people's feelings actually allowed? Must I simply learn how to become a good liar? If Mom and Dad break the rules, that means they are lying about what's okay and what's not okay—so maybe lying is what everybody does.

In one way or another, when a parent cheats it becomes very confusing for a child. He is left not only with the pain and disharmony in the family but also the confusion of trying to discern mixed messages and double standards regarding the all-important rules.

Stage 5

Since the adolescent stage is about developing one's identity, an important element of which is measuring oneself against one's parents, when there is parental infidelity, a young person's first question is: "Do I identify with the transgressor or the victim?" A person of this age may go back and forth from identifying with one to identifying with the other. If he identifies with the victim, he may harbor feelings of guilt for resenting the transgressor. Or he may feel guilty for having hurt the victim if he identifies with the transgressor. Either way, in his effort to discover who he is, the crisis of infidelity can interfere with a young person's healthy identity formation by creating a confusing choice of parental role models.

While the impact of parental infidelity varies according to a child's developmental stage, the consequences can be profound at any age. As you'll learn throughout the book, there are steps that parents and adult children can take to diminish the negative impact of a parent's unfaithfulness.

THE CONSEQUENCES OF
A BROKEN PROMISE

We live in a culture that encourages, even glorifies, individualism. We are taught that we deserve to have what we want and that we can get it if we want it badly enough. In other words, fulfilled desires equal personal satisfaction. Too often what are left out of this simple equation are the consequences affecting those who love us and depend on us. When a married parent secretly chooses to become sexually involved with another partner for whatever personal reasons—a sense of adventure, a physical or emotional yearning, an antidote to unhappiness with one's spouse or oneself—chances are that he or she has not considered how their children will be affected. Perhaps a parent believes that it is none of a child's business, that one's sex life is strictly personal. Or maybe a mother or father rationalizes infidelity with the commonly held belief that "children always learn to adapt."

Both of these assertions are true—to an extent. A parent's sexuality should not be the business of a son or daughter. But when that sexual behavior represents a broken promise that is at the heart of every family—the marriage vow of faithfulness—children are inadvertently involved. The rules have been broken, and children know it. They might be shielded from the truth about their parent's behavior, but they will likely find out at some point in their life, at which time the lie will be compounded for having been kept secret for so long.

It's true that children adapt. They will adjust to the reality of having a mother or father who had sex with someone else (or several "some-one elses"), and they will do what they can to get their needs met regardless of the fear, anger, confusion, disappointment, and loss of trust brought on by parental infidelity. Unfortunately, without the needed guidance or counseling, children of infidelity may adapt by engaging in a number of self-inhibiting behaviors: protecting them-selves from further disappointment by cutting themselves off from friends or opportunities, playing it safe by not opening themselves fully to friends or lovers, expecting less from love and from marriage, and/or seeking partners with whom they can replay the infidelity drama (either as the victim or the transgressor) to resolve or make sense of it.

Of course, this is not what parents want their children to go through. But children are generally not the focus when the decision is made to have an affair. What my clients and the hundreds of sur-vey respondents confirm, however, is that when the betrayer and the betrayed are also parents, marital infidelity is never a private affair.

In the next chapter, we'll explore what it means for a child of infi-delity to experience the loss of trust that is ushered in when one par-ent sexually betrays the other.

TWO

If I Can't Trust My Parent, Who Can I Trust?

The fact that my father, this man that I had put on a huge pedestal, cheated on my mother, a strong independent woman, has taken a huge toll on me. I no longer trust men at all. I have lost faith in my own child's father. Although he says he loves me, I do not trust him, or any man for that matter.

—*Female survey respondent in her early twenties*

My mother's affairs have given me great resentment toward women in general. I feel men always get blamed for being dogs, but my experience is women are far more deceiving.

—*Male survey respondent in his early thirties*

When one parent sexually betrays the other, a child's inner world and sense of the world at large are shattered. The personal environment in which he lives and from which he draws his sense of safety and security—namely, his family—is fundamentally changed because the most important people in that environment have become unrecognizable. The image of a mother or father who has sex with someone other than their spouse clashes with a child's or adult child's notion of what it means to be a husband or wife, and a parent. When this happens, the cheating parent can seem like a stranger, someone the child thought he knew but now discovers he doesn't. The parent is now seen as someone whose previous identity, before the cheating was discovered, was based on lies.

If a child can't trust that his parent is not a liar and will always be the person he purports to be, how can he trust that anyone else with whom he comes in contact is telling the truth? Given such doubts, children of infidelity may approach every personal interaction as suspect.

Kids not only feel as if they, too, have been betrayed by their cheating parent, they also wonder when the next betrayal will occur. In what other ways will the unfaithful parent lie or keep a secret? Perhaps the betrayed parent has also kept the secret of infidelity from the children, hoping to save them from emotional trauma, in which case that parent has become untrustworthy as well. When a father or mother has been caught in such a monumental lie, how can the child trust anything parents say or do? And in a broader sense, how can kids trust any grown-up who might only be pretending to live by the rules?

A child needs to be loved by his parents to develop a sense of self-worth, but when the love between his father and mother is sacrificed for a secret relationship outside the marriage, a child may identify with the betrayed parent and not trust that the betraying parent will always love him. Lacking in trust and becoming doubtful about love's staying power, some children of infidelity may feel the need to constantly please their parents and others to win the love they need.

Older children also develop problems with trust. Identifying with the betrayed parent, they may no longer believe that anyone could truly love them, because love seems conditional at best. They may feel that the betrayed parent must have made some mistake to warrant the infidelity, and they fear that they themselves might do something that will trigger a loved one's rejection and abandonment. To prevent their parent or others from betraying them, children of infidelity may think that they have to hide their emotions and be cautious about what they say and how they act. As they become adults and are involved in romantic relationships, they may avoid commitment for fear that getting too close to someone will make them vulnerable to betrayal. Or they may become overly suspicious and drive away a partner whom they unfairly believe is unfaithful.

In this chapter, we look at the repercussions of diminished trust through case histories of children and adult children whose parents were unfaithful. In each case, we'll explore what can happen when a parent's infidelity imparts the lesson that trusting those closest to you is too risky. At the end of the chapter, I'll offer advice for parents in an unfaithful marriage about repairing a child's ability to trust, as well as advice for adult children on developing their own sense of trust.

THE MANY FACES OF DIMINISHED TRUST

Regardless of the particular circumstances of a parent's infidelity, when a child of any age discovers that one parent has cheated on the other, kept it a secret, and lied about it, that child suffers a profound loss of trust. He can no longer take anyone at face value and thus constantly anticipates further betrayal. Among the survey respondents who shared with me their reactions to parental infidelity, there were many for whom loss of trust was the core issue. Before we explore the in-depth case histories in this chapter, I'd like you to take a look at the following comments from adult children of infidelity, ranging in age from twenty to fifty, for whom the feeling of "deep mistrust" is an ongoing and overriding issue.

- "After the cheating and my mother came back home, my brothers and I called her every hour to make sure she was where she said she was going to be. In my first relationship, I celebrated how many weeks I was with my boyfriend. I didn't trust that someone would stay around for very long." (Female, late twenties)
- "Both of my parents cheated on each other at different times of my life. My mother had an affair with [the man] who later became my stepfather, starting when I was three years old. I intuitively 'knew' about the infidelity, but it was later confirmed by my father. My father cheated on my stepmother many times, starting when I was in my teens, and they are still together. These infidelities created a deep sense of mistrust of men and a feeling of emptiness within me that has eroded my self-confidence and led me to believe that I was never enough. I am still struggling with these feelings." (Female, forties)
- "My father's infidelity affected me in so many ways—it definitely pulled my family apart. I hated the fact that relatives covered up for my father, and it caused me not to trust them as well—you never knew who was on your team, because while they appeared to love you, they were deceptive. Not only did it affect me growing up, but it also affected my self-esteem and fueled relationship fears. These fears included that my husband would cheat on me,

that I couldn't trust anybody to be there, that I couldn't rely on my family." (Female, late twenties)

- "I am constantly in a state of paranoia that my partner is cheating on me, lying to me, doing things behind my back that I will never know about. I will never look at my father the same way, and what little relationship we had before is nonexistent now. I don't believe in monogamy or that someone could be committed to one person for a lifetime. I don't really trust anyone anymore." (Female, early twenties)

- "It's hard to trust anyone, period. If your parents are capable of doing this to you, what is the rest of the world capable of?" (Female, early twenties)

Although the details of their infidelity stories vary, what each of these respondents share is the painfully unsettling experience of discovering that one of their parents sexually betrayed the other and thus broke one of the most important promises anyone can make. Because each of these children of infidelity felt they could no longer trust one or both parents, their ability to trust others was severely damaged as well.

In the following case history, Alicia reveals how the lack of trust engendered by her father's unfaithfulness continues to inform her adult relationships.

Alicia's Story: "I don't give people the opportunity to betray me."

A charismatic professional woman who enjoys both a successful career and a stable, happy marriage, Alicia's friendly, outgoing demeanor belies a lifelong distrust of people in general and men in particular. While she is warm and engaging in her professional relationships, in her personal life she has made it her policy to maintain an emotional distance from people until they have proven themselves trustworthy.

Alicia traces her continuing lack of trust to her father's infidelity, which she was made starkly aware of at the age of ten. Even before then, however, she knew her dad "liked the ladies." Here is how she tells it:

> *My father had always been a flirt. If there was ever a pretty woman in the room, he was the kind of man who would whistle at her or talk to her, even though his wife and daughters were right there. He would tell her how beautiful she was or how sexy she was, or say, "Do you want to dance with me, be my girlfriend?"—that kind of thing. When—hello!—his wife and children were right there. So my father was always somewhat inappropriate. He thought he was just being charming and flirtatious—and a man. But in my mind I always thought, Gee, I don't think he should be saying these things. He's a married man. Though I don't think I could have articulated it quite like that at such a young age.*

Even as a very young child, Alicia sensed the inappropriateness of her father's behavior, and it made her feel uncomfortable. Since hers was a family in which the husband and father was to be respected no matter what, neither Alicia's mother nor she and her sisters were allowed to show any disapproval of the man who was the head of their household. Perhaps the young daughters rationalized their dad's flirtatiousness by telling themselves he was only kidding around. After all, didn't some of the women to whom he made the remarks in restaurants and elsewhere find it flattering or amusing? But the discomfort Alicia had felt as a little girl was a signal of what lay ahead. On the day her father came home with startling news, Alicia's underlying emotional landscape changed forever.

When I was about ten, my father came home one day, sat us all down at the kitchen table, and announced to my mother and me and my sisters that we had a half sister named Tina and that she would be coming to live with us. She was two years older than me and the same exact age as my sister, Donna. None of us had known that such a person existed, and yet this girl was already twelve. My father told us that he was not happy with the way Tina's stepfather was raising her, so he was going to bring her into our family and raise her with us, because he thought that would be better for Tina.

Of course, we were all shocked. I think my mother had suspected but had never said anything. But we weren't encouraged to ask questions. My father was the authority, he was the father. He would make commands, and we would obey, because not only were we children, we were girls. So it wasn't our place to question him.

So he just came home and declared this, and we were like, "Okay." We weren't allowed to ask, "Well, how did this happen?" He simply told us, and we said okay. And then shortly thereafter he brought her home. My father had probably been unfaithful many, many times. But that was the one time that we had evidence of it, because there was a child. And so she came to live with us, and we had this living image of his betrayal of us— every day. We did our best to include her in the family, but it was hard. When I was old enough to do the math, I realized that while my mother was three months pregnant with Donna, my father was unfaithful to her and got another woman pregnant. And the result of that was Tina, my half sister.

I asked Alicia how she and her sisters reacted to the news that Tina would be joining the family, and she told me that they had to wait until they reached the safety of their bedroom to share with each other how they felt about the shocking evidence of their father's betrayal.

After we were given the news about having a half sister who would come to live with us, we were dismissed. We got up from the kitchen table, went to our bedroom, closed the door, and just started whispering to each other, "How did this happen?" We were so upset, we were just one raw bruise. We cried, but we couldn't cry too loud, because my father would have come in and smacked us. So we had to just kind of quietly commiserate with each other. And I think that was very indicative of our childhood. Our parents had their issues, their relationship, their marriage. They did their life in one way. And then we would go off into our bedroom and just cope with the hand we had been dealt. I can't remember what exactly we said to each other that day, but we just sat there on the bed and cried, and asked each other—"How could this happen? What does this mean? Who is this girl?"

Alicia said she felt her father had betrayed not only her mother but her and her sisters as well. After an initial teenage marriage that she says she escaped into to flee her family life, and which ended in divorce a few years later, Alicia dated only those men who were the exact opposite of her father. Not the charming or flirtatious ones who told her she was pretty or sexy, but the men who seemed more interested in what she had to say and in who she was as a person.

I was very aware that when it came to the men who I chose to date, I was deliberately choosing those who were the opposite of my father. Men who approached me with lines like, "Oh, you're so beautiful" or "You're so sexy—look at your eyes, look at that smile," I was thinking, "What do you want from me?—'cause you're not getting it." I was immediately cold to them, because that's my father's way. "Hey, sexy, hey gorgeous." Any man who approached me that way, I would just turn down.

A distrust of men led Alicia not only to choose an all-women's college but a mostly female-dominated profession as well. She concedes that these decisions derived primarily from her father's betrayal of the family. "I have very little patience for men," she told me, "and that's defined where I went to school, my career choice, and who I work with. I just wanted to have as little to do with men as possible." Although she has been happily married for more than seven years, and confesses that she chose her husband in part because he was nothing like her father, Alicia still cannot completely trust him. Her inability to trust completely, she says, manifests in the way she insists that she and her husband organize their financial affairs:

> *I think I trust women more than I've ever trusted a man. But I just don't trust people generally. Never having a bank account with my husband—I never have and never will—is directly because of my parents' relationship. Feeling that lack of security, that lack of trust. And that all comes from my father's betrayal.*

Her lack of trust extends to the way Alicia interacts with acquaintances and friends. She told me that she has devised a way of interacting with people that allows her to protect herself. She lets very few people get close, and those who do need to first prove themselves.

> *I never felt safe. And to this day I have very few friends. I can stand in front of a group and give a workshop or give a speech, and I can be very social and friendly. But I have very few people in my inner circle, people that I open my heart to. And the number one reason for that is trust. I do not trust people. There are very few people that I allow into my heart and into my personal life. My professional life is huge, but my personal life is small.*
>
> *To really be my friend, someone has to be persistent. They have to be the*

one to suggest getting together, to take the initiative. I'm very independent and I'm not very needy, but I think part of that is because I refuse to need people or depend on people, because if I do, what if they're not there for me? So I think part of my personality, and part of the way I handle relationships, is that I don't give people the opportunity to betray me or disappoint me. And a lot of this has to do with my family, my father specifically.

Alicia and her husband are now contemplating having children. When I asked her if she thought her husband might ever cheat on her, she told me that, while there are no assurances, she feels fairly confident he will be faithful; she told him when they'd been dating less than a year, "If you ever want to end this relationship, do one of two things: hit me or cheat on me. If you do either of those things, I'm gone." She does admit, however, that she enjoys flirting, but she would never carry anything further than friendliness. Now that she is on the brink of becoming a parent, Alicia says she could never betray a child like her father betrayed her and her family:

My father's infidelity has affected all areas of my life—my career, where I decided to go to college, my relationships with men . . . and I'm sure it will affect me as a mother; I'll be so conscious of raising a boy to respect women, and if it's a girl, raising her to demand respect from men. Everything that my father did, or should not have done, is going to affect me as a mother. If I'm unfaithful, I will be betraying my children, and that—even more than the fear of my husband finding out—would stop me. I want my children to love and admire me. I want to be worthy of being their mother. And a good mother does not cheat.

Matt's Story: "My mom has given me so many reasons why I can't trust her, and the infidelity is one of them."

As Alicia's story revealed, sometimes a daughter's or son's experience with parental infidelity serves as an indelible example of what not to seek in a relationship. In Matt's case, his mother's lack of trustworthiness was so pronounced that he sought a mate who was her extreme opposite. Being able to implicitly trust the person with whom he would share his life would be of prime importance to Matt, precisely because his mother had kept so many secrets and had betrayed her family for so many years.

Throughout his childhood, Matt and his siblings had witnessed their parents' acrimonious relationship, but it wasn't until after his parents split up, when he was nineteen years old, that Matt found out about his mother's ongoing extramarital affair.

My parents never got along very well. They fought a lot, really violently a lot—not to the point of hitting but a lot of yelling and screaming and breaking things. So that was pretty unpleasant for all of us, and then they finally went their separate ways. They had tried to wait until my youngest brother was out of high school, but they didn't make it that far.

After they divorced, I was home from my first year of college spending some time with my mom, and I was kind of wondering why she hadn't started dating yet now that she was single, because she had always been very outgoing, while my dad was much more shy and introverted. So I asked her, and she said, "Well, actually, there is somebody that I'm in love with." And just out of my mouth, without thinking at all, I said, "Oh . . . is it that guy named Stan?" and she confirmed that it was.

Although Matt told me that he had not known when he was growing up that his mother was having an affair, it seems that somewhere inside of himself, he had known something was going on even when he was a very young boy. The man his mother had apparently carried on with for years was someone who had stuck in Matt's mind since he was about five years old: "This was a person my father had worked with when I was a little kid, and one of my earliest memories was of our two families getting together at his house. I guess it had struck me as unusual, because my parents didn't socialize much as a couple, probably because they were so unhappy together, and this was one of those rare times. So I remembered this guy from a very early childhood memory—and then fourteen or fifteen years later his name just flew out of my mouth, completely unbidden. So on some level, I must have known about my mom's relationship with him."

When I asked him how things changed with his mother after he found out about her extramarital affair with Stan, Matt told me that his relationship with her had never been a very good one. The infidelity seemed to confirm what he had always known—she was someone he couldn't trust: "The infidelity was one behavior pattern, but she's really very dishonest about a lot of things. My mom has given me so many reasons why I can't trust her, and the infidelity is one of them. The fact that she could keep a relationship secret for that long, that she kept seeing this person the whole time my parents were married. I'm not sure how often, but they kept the relationship going throughout my parents' marriage."

Aside from the secret relationship with Stan, Matt's mother had still more secrets that she had kept from her family. It wasn't until Matt was in his early thirties that he found out his mother had had a child with another man while she was married to Matt's dad. "She just kind of sprung it on me, totally out of the blue, that I had an older sister. She told my brothers and sisters and I when it was convenient for her, because she felt like she needed sympathy from us.

But it wasn't a conscious decision like, 'I think it's time to tell everybody about this.' [This was just one more instance of her being very manipulative and kind of pathologically dishonest."

So how did his mother's infidelity and long-held secrets affect Matt's ability to trust in his own adult relationships? Given the same family history, other young men may have had a very tough time ever being able to fully trust a partner. Matt told me that his happy marriage is the result of knowing what he needed from a woman to create a successful relationship—even though that "knowing" may have been on an unconscious level.

> *I think probably not even on a conscious level, trustworthiness was something I really looked for. My wife is pretty much 180 degrees from my mom; I can trust her completely. But I don't know if I would have told you that that was one of the traits I was looking for if we had had this conversation before I was in a relationship.*

Another significant aspect to Matt's story is that he doesn't hold his mother's inability to be faithful against women in general, as others in our survey have done with regard to their parent's infidelity. "I don't generalize my mom's behavior to all women, because she is quite different from most of the women I've encountered, even ones who have been unfaithful—there hasn't been that level of dishonesty."

Matt admitted that the temptation to be unfaithful is not something he is entirely free of. But knowing firsthand how infidelity can tear apart a family's trust, he has incorporated the lessons learned into his current behavior:

> *That dynamic of my parents is always kind of an example of what I don't want to have happen. Being married twelve years, there's always a temptation, but I always ask myself, "Is a particular attraction really*

genuine?" It helps me identify that I should really be working on things
with my wife rather than looking elsewhere. Looking elsewhere seems like
the easiest thing to do.

It seems that "looking elsewhere" was the way Matt's mother dealt
with the unhappiness in her marriage. The fact that she kept secrets
from Matt's father and from the rest of the family caused Matt to distrust her, even when he was a child and didn't know exactly what was
going on in her life. Being unable to trust his mother was an ongoing
feature of Matt's relationship with her, but he fortunately didn't reas-
sign that lack of trust to other women. He was able to objectively perceive women on their own merits and to choose a life mate who is
well deserving of his trust.

The following case history reflects what can happen when a child
of infidelity's ability to trust is more severely damaged.

Linda's Story: "When I was eleven, I swore I'd never let a man be unfaithful to me."

Linda remembers the night that everything irrevocably changed for
her and her family. She was eleven. Her parents had always been very
close and loving, but lately her mother, who was pregnant at the time,
had suspected that something was wrong. Linda's father had been
going out a lot at night, giving the excuse that his wife shouldn't come
along because of her condition. But on this particular night, Linda's
mother decided to follow her husband. She got into a taxi, and when
it approached her husband's car at a red light, she got out of the taxi,
opened her husband's car door, and found a woman in the passenger
seat. Her husband simply took off, with the car door open—not both-
ering to confront his wife or even to close the car door.

Linda's mother felt so humiliated she went into a rampage when her husband finally arrived home that night. Linda was there to witness the blowup. She relates,

My mom was sitting on the sofa waiting for my father for what seemed like hours. She didn't move, just sat there staring straight ahead. I sat near her, and for some reason, I focused on the little white stones that were in one of the potted plants. When my father finally came home three or four hours later, my mom picked up a huge plant and threw it at him. I remember seeing him with all those little white rocks in his hair and on his clothes. That night my mom took me with her to a hotel. I swore to myself that night that I'd never let a man be unfaithful to me.

Linda told me that, at the time, she didn't have an emotional reaction to what happened that night. While she waited with her mother for her father to come home, while she looked on as her mother became enraged and threw the plant, as she witnessed her father strewn with the white stones, and while she listened to the two of them screaming at each other, it was like watching a soap opera, she said. Her emotions were frozen; instead of feeling anything, she experienced the events as a mere spectator. Linda was the audience for her parent's infidelity drama, but she was much more than a bystander. Although she wasn't consciously aware of it, she sensed that she had to keep her own emotions hidden to be strong for her mom and help protect her. She also made a secret vow to herself: that she would never allow a man to do to her what her father had done to her mother.

There was no way Linda could protect her mother from the painful consequences of her father's infidelity. He continued to live with her mom—professing his love for her—but he also continued having affairs. Linda's mother was always in doubt as to her husband's whereabouts, always suspicious of the time he spent away from home. She would accuse him, and he would deny the accusations. But the fact was that he had a mistress in another town for more than ten years.

Because Linda's mother could never prove that her suspicions were valid, she felt like she was going crazy. And she became extremely depressed. She died in her early forties of cancer, and Linda believes that her mom's long-term suffering over her father's many betrayals contributed to her illness and ultimately to her death.

It was only years later that Linda realized how great an impact her father's lies and infidelity had on her own life. The minute she discovered that her first husband had been unfaithful to her, she kept the promise she had made to herself when she was eleven. She banished him from her life forever. "I erased him from my life. I left him without even giving him any explanation. The only thing I gave him was a divorce." All the pent-up anger Linda had felt toward her father for betraying her mother was unleashed on her husband for betraying her.

Linda now wonders if she might have dealt with her own marital situation differently. Perhaps she and her husband could have gone for counseling to consider whether they might have been able to work things out. She now recognizes that by repressing her emotional reactions to her father's betrayal, she was forced to deal with those charged emotions later. It's even possible that she chose a partner who was likely to betray her, so that she would have the opportunity to express those angry feelings that were initiated when she was eleven.

After a second divorce, Linda had a number of relationships but none that lasted very long. She says her intention was to be in a lasting relationship, but whenever she felt there was the slightest chance that the guy might be the type to be unfaithful, she broke it off. She admitted that she would get involved with a man too quickly, and then she would leave too quickly at the first sign of conflict. She says that now she has a "pretty good" relationship with someone who lives thousands of miles away, but they only see each other once a year.

An inability to trust any man she becomes involved with is at the core of Linda's relationships. Whether a husband or a more casual boyfriend, in her mind every man is a potential cheater whom she can never fully trust. She has become so fearful of going through what her mother experienced that whenever she's in a relationship that she thinks will make her happy—or when something doesn't go the way she thinks it should—she runs away. A part of her has still not been able to come to terms with that eleven-year-old's trauma.

Linda is committed to overcoming the legacy of her parents' infidelity scenario. She wants to have a closer, more trusting relationship with her long-distance boyfriend, and to that end they have both agreed to spend more time together. She is looking forward to some point soon when they can live in the same city and see where dating each other on a steadier basis might lead. Linda has come to realize that to have a more intimate relationship with a man, she must feel safe enough to work out the inevitable conflicts that arise in every relationship. She can't do that at an emotional—or physical—distance, but she is determined to break through that resistance. I am helping Linda to recognize that just because she inherited a lack of trust as a child of infidelity doesn't mean she'll never be able to trust her partner. Establishing that trust not only requires choosing someone trustworthy but also understanding her experience of parental infidelity and then letting go of it.

Linda learned from her parents' marital problems that partners can be untrustworthy and love can be painful. In response, she has engaged in a pattern of self-protection by avoiding intimacy or running away when a relationship gets too close. But she can never love or be loved by employing this kind of protection. It would be like expecting to be nourished while avoiding food, because you once ate something poisonous. Linda is in the process of letting go of the pain she and her mother endured years ago. And she is also learning to forgive her father by seeing him as a man who did not hurt his family intentionally. His motivation for having affairs may have been his narcissism, social pressure, his own family history, or other factors.

Linda is discovering that her father acted according to his various psychological drives, as did her mother, and that like all humans, they both made mistakes. Although Linda's lack of trust derives from her experience with parental infidelity, she needn't live with the psychological fallout any longer. Once she can forgive her father (for more on forgiveness, see Chapter 8), let go of the past, and separate her current experiences with men from the trauma she experienced as an eleven-year-old girl, Linda will be free to trust and to love.

Tom's Story: "I never wanted to see my mother again— and I never want a woman in my life."

Tom's story is an extreme case. I present it in the hope that it will shed a stark light on how deeply children can be affected by the lies associated with parental infidelity—and why it is so important for both children and adult children to rebuild their ability to trust before it's too late.

Now forty-one, Tom was only four when his father abandoned the family for reasons Tom wouldn't learn about for another ten years. When Tom was fourteen, his older brother died in a car accident, and it was only then that Tom found out that this brother was actually a half brother. He was the product of an affair Tom's mother had had. In fact, she had had a series of affairs throughout her marriage to Tom's dad, and another of Tom's siblings was also the result of one of her extramarital sexual relationships. It was at this time that Tom finally discovered that his mother's ongoing infidelity was what had driven his father away when Tom was four.

The news of his deceased brother's true identity, his mother's repeated infidelity, and the true reason for his father's departure was so disturbing for the teenaged Tom that it caused him to begin planning his permanent escape from the family. Confronted with the facts surrounding his mother's sexual infidelities, he questioned his own identity and that of his mother as well. Although she had always had boyfriends after Tom's father had left, the person Tom had thought she was no longer existed; she had become someone whom Tom now considered despicable. When he was sixteen, as soon as he was able to secure a job and move out of his mother's home, Tom left. He remembers his mother asking, "Where are you going?" to which he replied, "None of your business." As he put it, he "abandoned" his family and went to live on his own.

It was clear to me that Tom used the word "abandoned" because he now identified with his father having abandoned the family upon discovering his wife's unfaithfulness. As soon as Tom discovered the truth behind the lies he had grown up with, he desperately wanted to avoid contact with his entire family. As he tells it, he simply couldn't bear to be around his mother and to think about the sexual behavior she had engaged in. When he left home at sixteen, it was the last time he ever saw her. "I didn't want anything to do with her at all," he told me, "and I still don't."

When he turned eighteen, Tom joined the army, which he said was the best thing he could have done for himself. He learned how to live within a structure and how to create a life for himself. There had been little structure in Tom's family when he was growing up. He was raised with the concept that parents do whatever they want. His mother had affairs whenever she wanted to, and his father, according to Tom, was a weak man who simply left the family when a crisis hit—never to show up again.

Tom followed in his father's footsteps by leaving his family behind. Although he is interested in women sexually, Tom has never had a girl-friend, never been married, and he never wants anything to do with women at all. He says that he's fine living by himself. Decades after his mother's infidelity was brought to light, he made it a point to state adamantly in our interview, "I never want a woman in my life."

Sadly, there was no role model with whom Tom could identify as a youngster. The only choice he was able to make was to identify with his father (whom he only remembers from pictures) and to take the same action that he had: leave home. While Tom says that he considers his father a weak person for abandoning the family, he also concedes that it was the best his father could do under the circumstances.

No longer in the army, Tom now works as a bouncer in a strip club. He tells me he continues to feel distant from and angry toward women. Having learned from his parents that he can never trust a woman, Tom seems condemned to a lonely life. But is it possible that it's not too late for Tom to learn to trust?

TRUST IS A NEED AND A FEELING— BUT ALSO A LEARNABLE SKILL

To develop emotional security, a baby needs to trust that his parents will feed, nurture, love, and care for him. If his parents provide that necessary love and caretaking, the baby feels an essential sense of trust, which will in turn enable him to trust other people and the world in general. So in this primal way, trust is both a crucial need and an empowering feeling.

When there is infidelity between parents, and a child learns that the most important people in his world are untrustworthy, his ability to trust others can be seriously impaired, as we have witnessed in the stories throughout this chapter. A child of infidelity who is lacking in trust often assumes that a friend, partner, or spouse will betray him. He may be overly suspicious, emotionally distant, or refrain from committing to a relationship because he cannot trust that the other person will act honorably and really be there for him. Because he lacks an essential sense of trust, and because he doesn't want to get hurt in the way that he witnessed his parent or parents being hurt, a child of infidelity does whatever it takes to protect himself from being emotionally vulnerable.

So is it possible for such a person to relearn how to trust? I believe that it is. I believe that trust is a need and a feeling, but also a skill that can be learned. Even when a child has been subjected to parental infidelity and feels that he cannot trust anybody, even though he has suffered the betrayal and confusion that seriously affect a child's or an adult child's faith in himself and others, there is a process that he can go through to learn how to trust.

The first step in that process is to acknowledge our need to trust. We need to trust to feel safe, to develop and express ourselves, and to give and receive love. A young child needs to trust that there is someone—or, hopefully, more than one person—on whom he can rely to provide structure and to be there for him unconditionally. Without that sense of security, a child is afraid and tentative. An older child or young adult needs to trust to develop healthy relationships and the sense of security that allows him to fulfill his goals. Admitting to yourself that you need to trust others to be emotionally healthy paves the way for being able to do so.

Even if you were raised in a family where parental infidelity gravely damaged your sense of trust, you can learn to assess the trustworthiness of those you may want in your life, which is the second step in the process of reestablishing a sense of trust. You can learn to make a wise choice about who you're going to trust and to what degree. Children of infidelity may feel that no one is to be trusted. If Mom was the cheating parent, as in Tom's case, all women may be deemed untrustworthy. If Dad was the cheater, as in Alicia's case, all men may be viewed as potential liars and cheaters until proven otherwise. But even those who have been terribly betrayed by their parents can come to understand that there are those who are trustworthy and those who aren't. Maybe you can trust certain people completely and others you can trust only in specific circumstances.

In fact, many of the children of infidelity whom I interviewed for this book conceded that their parent who cheated was still trustworthy in some way. "Even though he was a cheater and I could never trust that he wouldn't do it again, I did trust that he loved me and that he wanted me to be happy. And that he cared about my career and my future," one woman told me. She had found out about her father's unfaithfulness when she was sixteen and had a very difficult time trusting men throughout her twenties and early thirties, but she had to admit that she did trust that her father cared about her. I think it's important for children of infidelity to acknowledge that trustworthiness is not all black and white. You may not be able to trust your parent, friend, or partner to be 100 percent honest all the time, or to be there for you in every way, but in thinking about your relationship with that person, you can determine if they are trustworthy enough to remain in your life—or not. While it is crucial to have people in your life whom you can trust, you would only be hurting yourself if you allowed yourself to trust everyone unconditionally.

As a child of infidelity, you might look back and determine that neither of your parents was trustworthy, but perhaps there was a grandparent, an uncle, a neighbor, or a teacher—someone who taught you that there are people who are worthy of your trust. By reflecting on that trustworthy person—someone with whom you could be emotionally honest and who was there for you—you can begin the process of opening yourself to other trustworthy people. Even if you no longer have contact with that person from your past, he or she can inspire you to begin to trust others from now on.

Children of infidelity need to remind themselves that they always have the option to trust, even when that trust was shattered by a parent. You don't have to trust everyone, but you don't have to distrust everybody either. You can make the decision to be trusting of those who deserve your trust. Again, there is a skill to learning how to trust, and figuring out who you can trust is part of this learning process. Relationships with parents, friends, acquaintances, schoolmates, coworkers, romantic partners, and others provide you with experiences in trustworthiness. Being aware of the ways in which others demonstrated or failed to demonstrate their ability to make you feel respected, listened to, and safe will help you hone your skill at choosing who to trust.

As a child of infidelity reading this book, you are becoming aware of how your inability to trust has affected your relationships. If you ask yourself how you feel when you distrust someone, and look at the arguments you give yourself about why you distrust that person, you may hear the inner voices of your mother or your father—or your own voice as a child when you discovered the infidelity of one of your parents.

It's important to recognize that there is often a fine line between correctly assessing someone's untrustworthiness and generalizing that this person must be untrustworthy because all men are or all women are (because your parent was) or all married people are (because your parents were). If you distrust everybody, you're not giving yourself the opportunity to receive the understanding, support, and love that others may want to give you. If you always suspect a secret agenda, you may need to give yourself time to go through the process of reestablishing trust.

Each person goes through this process at his or her own pace, and it cannot be rushed. Genuinely trusting someone takes time, as does earning someone's trust. You might begin by assessing how the person responds when you've trusted him with a minor issue. Does he come through for you and prove his loyalty, or disappoint you and leave you guessing as to where his loyalties lie? You can also take note of how this person demonstrates his trustworthiness with others. Does he behave honorably, morally, and loyally toward his other friends and family members? If he is not loyal to those people, he's likely not going to be loyal in your relationship either. So it's important to assess how someone demonstrates his trustworthiness; then, when you feel ready, you can show your own intention to be loyal and trustworthy.

If you are too reserved in offering your trust, the other person will likely be that way, too. Or you may open up, and he may take more time, because everyone comes to a relationship with his or her own issues. But learning to trust has to be a healthy balance between openness and caution, offering and accepting. And there's always the chance that trust between two people may never develop. If you've given yourself time to build trust with someone and it is not developing, it may be a sign that the person is undeserving of your trust.

Relearning how to trust as a child of infidelity involves one more step: understanding why your parent was unfaithful. This is a very difficult step for adolescents, who lack the life experience to put their parent's behavior in perspective, and it is almost impossible for young children, who expect their parents to be perfect. But a mature adolescent or an adult child of infidelity can consider their parent's behavior and determine the valid reasons for why it may have happened. This doesn't mean justifying parental infidelity; it means looking at the behavior in a more objective light. Perhaps your parents had serious marital conflicts that led one spouse to seek validation or comfort in another partner; maybe the cheating parent was himself a child of infidelity and unconsciously modeled his behavior after his unfaithful mother or father; or perhaps your parent used affairs to prop up a sagging ego.

In putting forth the effort to try to understand your parents, and recognizing that they have their own frailties and emotional injuries, you may come to realize that each of us is on a life path in search of what we need to feel whole, and that we often create crises with the person who is closest to us to resolve past issues. Understanding what happened between your parents is crucial in preventing you from "acting out" your loss of trust within your own relationships. Instead of sabotaging your own happiness by engaging in self-defeating behavior, you can learn to be more open and more trusting with appropriate individuals by acknowledging the need to trust, giving yourself time to assess the trustworthiness of a particular friend or partner, and developing an understanding of why your parent was unfaithful in the first place.

REBUILDING YOUR CHILD'S TRUST
(For Parents in an Unfaithful Marriage)

Once sexual infidelity has affected your family, you'll need to face the issues of honesty and credibility with your children. This will not be easy, because regardless of your children's ages, they are likely to feel upset, confused, angry, and disappointed in you and/or your spouse.

And, depending on whether you are the betrayed or the betrayer, talking with your kids about something this personal can be embarrassing, belittling, or shameful. Still, when parents attempt to justify their lie or their inappropriate behavior, things can get tricky, because this often leads to yet another lie—and a child's continued lack of trust. Although it is the betrayer who owes the family an explanation for his or her infidelity, it is the betrayed parent who is most likely to talk with the children about what happened and why. Whichever parent attempts to explain parental infidelity, children may not always find the explanations satisfactory and can continue to feel upset and confused. This is because the betrayed parent may provide an explanation that includes his or her own resentments, or he/she may try to justify the spouse's infidelity to placate the child, which could actually exacerbate the child's anger. Still, it is necessary to provide some kind of explanation as a sign of respect for your child; not providing one will be even more emotionally damaging.

So how might you approach the subjects of infidelity, honesty, and credibility with your young child, adolescent, or adult child to begin the process of rebuilding trust? If you are the betrayer, you might say something like this to your young child: "I am very sorry for the pain that I am causing you and your mom/dad. I behaved in a selfish manner because I only thought of myself—and not how much your mother/father and you would be hurt. I kept the relationship with someone else a secret because I did not want you to be ashamed of me. I am ashamed of myself now. I will do everything possible to make it up to you, but there is one thing that I want to assure you: I love you, and as your parent I will do my best to never disappoint you. Sometimes things happen between adults, and even when we are grown-ups, we do not handle ourselves in the best way. I am learning from this mistake, and I promise to exercise better judgment from now on."

Of course, you need to mean what you say and hold yourself to such a statement. Your promise to your children and your plan of action will depend on your particular circumstances. You may be in the wrong relationship and may decide to end the marriage, or you may decide to work on your marriage by going to counseling or by employing some other means. In either case, be mindful of the fact that lies and betrayal are affecting your children, and their ability to trust you and others with whom they'll have relationships is dependent on how you handle the current crisis.

If you are the betrayer and your child is a preteen, teen, or young adult, your statement to him might be similar to the previous one, but with an added focus on how difficult adult relationships can be: "Relationships between adults are not always easy. I realize that I broke a commitment to your mother/father, and that I should have faced the problems in our relationship rather than creating more serious ones. Instead of working on our differences, I turned to a distraction. If it turns out that our marriage problems can't be solved, your mother/father and I will need to make decisions together, but lying or deceiving is not an option, and it will not be my option anymore. I hope you can trust me, because I now trust myself to stick to my word."

If you are the betrayed parent, you might say something like this to your young child: "Sometimes grown-ups act in a way that surprises their children. I am also hurt by your mother's/father's behavior, but this is something that he/she and I will discuss and work out. Together, we will try to make the best decisions possible. I know that your mother/father did not mean to hurt you because she/he loves you very much."

And you might say something like this to a preteen, teen, or young adult: "Although what your mom/dad did was wrong, I know that she/he did not mean to hurt us. He/she and I will work out between us what this means for our relationship and where we'll go from here, but whatever happens between us, I know that he/she will prove to you that he/she loves you very much."

Your child needs to know that he can trust you. Any further lies will only reinforce his loss of trust. However you choose to assure your child that you and your spouse will be truthful from now on, honorable actions speak louder than your words. Usually after a crisis like parental infidelity, family dynamics change. If you use this difficult time to become more honest and open with your children, they will learn from your example about the importance of trust, and you will be giving them a priceless gift—the ability to trust—which is an essential element in any healthy relationship.

THREE

Why Do I Feel So Ashamed?

Most of my friends knew about what was happening at home, but I didn't want to talk about it or answer their stupid questions. What my mom did was disgusting, so why would I want to talk about it with anybody?

—*Zack, twenty-three (referring to how he felt at thirteen)*

I remember telling friends how upset I was that my dad had cheated on my mom with women who were almost as young as me. Almost across the board, the guys would say things like, "Wow, good for him! Sounds like my kind of guy." In their eyes his behavior was cool. One of my closest girlfriends made a comment about my father needing what my mom obviously couldn't give him. It was horribly humiliating.

—*Rachel, twenty-five*

I don't remember her ever saying, "Don't tell your dad"—
I just didn't. People in the family knew and didn't say anything.
So I felt dirty and ashamed.

—*Ellen, thirty (referring to how she felt at twelve)*

Children are often overwhelmed by feelings of shame when a parent's infidelity is discovered. Neighbors, classmates, and friends want to know, "Why did your dad (or mom) leave?" or "Why is your mom always crying?" thus pressuring kids to divulge information that deeply embarrasses them. Or, they may lie to save face and keep the secret about what's really going on between their mother and father. Sixty-two percent of our survey respondents said they felt ashamed or embarrassed to talk to their friends and others about their parents' infidelity.

Even though the actions of their parents are clearly not their responsibility, children of infidelity bear the burden of shame when one parent cheats on the other. They wonder, "What will my friends think of my father (or mother) now? What will they think of me?" They may even feel uncomfortable around extended family members who are supportive but who, kids sense, might be talking behind their backs about the dishonorable behavior of their parent.

Young children generally look upon their parents through admiring eyes. They view their mother and father as models for respectable behavior who make decisions based on what is correct and proper. But when a parent has an affair and is referred to by the other spouse—as well as by other people within and outside the family— as a "cheater," a child is not only confused but ashamed. There is a very clear negative resonance to the word "cheater," even if a young child doesn't understand the context of the parent's cheating. A cheater is not someone a young child can feel proud of, and young children want to feel proud of their parents. A preschool or elementary school-age child is unable to view his father or mother as a person with insecurities and self-doubts, as a flawed individual who sometimes makes mistakes. So when one parent is chastised by the other for being unfaithful—whatever word is used to describe that behavior—a young child is left with the discomforting image of that parent as a bad person.

Since young children tend to think of themselves as being the center of their world, they may feel somehow responsible for the parent's wrongdoing and thus ashamed of themselves. They might search for a reason that would explain why their parent sought love from another man or woman. A little girl might feel that her temper tantrums caused her mother to seek a boyfriend instead of staying at home with her father. Or perhaps a young son feels there was something he could have done to prevent his father from getting involved with a girlfriend. Maybe he could have said something to his dad that would have convinced him not to hurt his mother this way. A young girl, while identifying with her betrayed mother's pain, may feel that if she herself had been more loving toward her father, he would not have needed to find love outside the home. Whatever explanation a young child of infidelity comes up with, it likely reflects the age-appropriate notion that everything in his life revolves around him. So if Dad cheats on Mom or Mom has a boyfriend, a child figures it must somehow be his own fault, which causes feelings of guilt and shame.

For older children, teens, and young adults, a sense of shame is often brought on by the comments and attitudes of others. While they're old enough to be aware of sexual issues and to assume that infidelity is a fact of life, they still find it very difficult to see their own parents as human beings who might "fall out of love" or be tempted by the affections of another partner. They don't want to think about their parents as sexual beings, and being forced to imagine a parent having sex with someone other than the other parent is even more upsetting. When older children of infidelity describe how they felt when they found out that their father or mother was having an affair, they often use words ranging from shocked and disillusioned to disgusted. And when they had to confront people outside of the family with the reality of their parent's behavior, many children of infidelity reported feeling embarrassed, humiliated, ashamed, and disgraced.

In this chapter we'll hear from those whose overriding response to a parent's unfaithfulness was shame, and we'll talk about how feelings of shame and guilt can affect a child of infidelity's self-esteem. We'll also discuss the burden of guilt that children carry when they have to either keep the secret of their parent's adultery or divulge that secret.

Later in the chapter, we'll explore how a child of any age deals with the fact that a parent's adulterous behavior contradicts his or her professed moral values. I'll advise parents how to help younger children deal with the issues of shame and hypocrisy, and I'll discuss how older children of infidelity can confront their own sense of embarrassment, humiliation, and shame. But first let's consider how it feels to be publicly shamed for something you didn't do.

PUBLIC HUMILIATION

Jennifer's father is a college professor. During her sophomore year, she decided to take a class he was teaching since it was a required course and he had the reputation for being one of the best professors in the department. Unfortunately, along with listening to his brilliant lectures, Jennifer had to witness her dad in action—flirting with female students after class, causing her intense embarrassment. She realized that she should have anticipated how he might behave and how it would make her feel, as her dad had never confined his flirtations to the classroom; he had a habit of making suggestive remarks to family friends, waitresses, salesclerks, and Jennifer's girlfriends as well. "What's up with your dad?" one friend had asked Jennifer when she was still in high school, "why doesn't he hit on women his own age?"

As Jennifer soon found out, her dad had indulged in behavior that went beyond flirtation and verbal harassment; in fact, it would eventually cost him his tenured position at the college. He had had a series of affairs with students beginning when Jennifer was a child. She just hadn't found out about them until she was in college herself. Jennifer's mother had apparently put up with her husband's infidelity to keep the family together, but Jennifer felt the full measure of humiliation when her father's improprieties became campus news. Her father's affair with a coed was cause for his dismissal when the young woman's parents found out about the relationship and reported him to the administration. Of course, Jennifer was devastated. She had always known her father was a flirt, but she had never presumed that he carried his flirtations any further. Publicly humiliated, Jennifer felt she could no longer tolerate going to the college where her father's affair was known to everyone. She dropped out of school, moved away, and spent nearly a year in therapy before she finally felt ready to apply to another school and get on with her life.

Unfortunately, parents who cheat rarely consider how their children might be affected. Even high-profile parents like former president Bill Clinton, former governor Eliot Spitzer, and former mayor Rudolph Giuliani didn't seem to bear in mind how their children would be hurt by their infidelities. Nonetheless, once their sexual indiscretions become news, some politicians take umbrage at

unfaithful to their spouse, we may be disappointed or we may conclude that "everyone seems to engage in extramarital affairs, so what's the big deal?" But regardless of how we perceive a public figure's behavior, or how common such behavior has become, is the embarrassment and shame that is likely felt by their children any less?

When Rudolph Giuliani was mayor of New York City, his public flaunting of his extramarital affair with the woman who would later become his wife caused his estrangement from his young adult daughter and son. Four years after Giuliani married his lover, his college-age son, Andrew, was quoted as saying, "There's obviously a little problem that exists between me and his wife. And we're trying to figure that out. But as of right now it's not working as well as we would like." No one asked Andrew Giuliani whether he felt ashamed of his father, or whether it was embarrassing for him to have to state why he was estranged from his dad, but knowing how other children of infidelity have felt in similar situations, I would speculate that Andrew probably felt humiliated about something he had absolutely nothing to do with.

While children of public figures whose parents are caught having affairs may experience public humiliation, even children of infidelity who are not in the public eye often face the inquisitive stares, probing remarks, and off-color comments among their friends and family. They, too, are familiar with what Chelsea Clinton and Andrew Giuliani went through. Their sense of shame may not be as public, but it can be just as tough to weather.

Rachel's Story: "My father's sleazy life reflects on me."

At twenty-five, Rachel is a young woman who considers herself both realistic and worldly. She told me that when she was growing up, many of her friends' parents had been divorced, and the issue of infidelity was not unknown to her. But when Rachel's mother found out that Rachel's dad had been having affairs for the last ten years of their twenty-eight-year marriage, Rachel was stunned. The person she had known her father to be seemed to have vanished, and in his place was a "despicable womanizer whose actions disgusted me."

Rachel had always been proud of her dad. He was a respected architect, charming, likable, and intelligent. She had taken pride in introducing her friends to both her parents.

But now my father was this creepy guy who had snuck around on my mom. He'd had a thing with his assistant, with a young woman who taught a class at his health club, and others that he met in his secret life outside our home. His lowlife behavior smeared our whole family. I was his daughter, so how could it not reflect on me?

When Rachel began confiding in her closest friends that her father's affairs had caused her and her sister (not to mention their mom) a great deal of emotional pain, she expected sympathy; instead, she was met with comments she describes as "horribly humiliating." She was twenty-two when her father's infidelity was discovered, but three years later she still feels the sense of shame and humiliation that she felt initially. Several conversations in particular stick in her mind:

I remember talking to one of my best friends about it, and she told me that I was naive to think that most married people don't cheat. She said that my mother must not have been satisfying my dad's sexual needs, that middle-aged men need to be with a younger woman in order to make them feel more alive, and that the affairs could even benefit my parents' marriage. I couldn't believe that my best friend not only had the nerve to analyze my parents' sex life but was basically defending the disgusting way my father had treated my mom! How could she not know how horrible it felt to have an entirely different man for a father—one who made me ashamed to be related to him? She was basically telling me that what my dad did was perfectly normal and that I was just being childish by getting all upset about it.

Then there were my guy friends who told me they thought it was "cool" that my dad had had an affair with his assistant and the girl in the health club, both of whom were close to my age. I consider myself just as open-minded as anyone else, but I can't tell you how sleazy it felt having these guys talk about my father like that.

Rachel's shame was intensified by her mother's experiences in the initial months following her father's coming clean about his "secret life." Her mom would run into a neighbor or friend, and now that the news of her husband's indiscretions was out in the open, these women felt free to recount how he had come on to them at a party or how they had heard that so-and-so had also had an affair with him. Hearing about her husband's sexual escapades directly from him was bad enough; hearing more details from friends and neighbors compounded the humiliation. Since Rachel's mom shared the unwelcome gossip with her daughters, this only added to Rachel's feelings of shame.

I'd be out somewhere and bump into friends of my parents who would talk as if nothing had happened but would give me this look. Nothing was said outright about my father, but it was implicit in their look. A sly kind of grin or an expression of pity—the point was that they knew. And I knew they knew. And it made me feel horrible. Again, his sleazy behavior was now part of how people looked at me. Part of what they saw when they saw me.

As Rachel soon learned, we come to realize who our most sensitive friends are during a time of crisis. Those who are most helpful are the ones who know how to listen and support us. Others may not mean us any harm, but due to their lack of maturity or perhaps their own unresolved issues, their remarks can hurt our feelings and make us feel humiliated or ashamed. Young people can often find it very difficult to understand the emotional pain of a family in crisis, and they may blurt out something that they think is helpful when in fact such remarks make a child of infidelity feel much worse about the turmoil that's going on between her parents.

Also, adolescents and young adults (and older adults as well) can be attracted to gossip. Young people in particular may contribute to gossip as a way to enhance their popularity, since at this stage of their lives social pressure often influences their behavior. In the case of some of Rachel's friends, the urge to engage in gossip may have caused their insensitive comments. Others might have been reacting to their own family issues. For example, what did Rachel know about the upbringing of those male friends whose remarks caused her to feel so humiliated? Had they been raised to believe that married men are "cool" for having affairs with young women? And were they taught that it is also cool for married women to have affairs with young men? Probably not. They may have been raised by chauvinistic fathers, however. Or perhaps there was marital discord in their homes, which led them to believe that a married man having an affair would be acceptable and justified.

It is important to take into account where our friends are coming from. While we are usually too emotionally vulnerable during a crisis to objectively analyze why a friend might be making a particular remark, we should realize that we can open ourselves to hurt feelings if we expect support from those who are unable to offer it. We can usually sense immediately if someone is not in tune with what we're going through, and instead of opening ourselves to hurt feelings, we can consciously choose to distance ourselves from that person.

As Rachel was forced to discover, children of parents who cheat are often obliged to walk a path strewn with insensitive remarks that only add to their sense of hurt and shame. Unfortunately, there is no way you can take a shortcut around such a path. What you can do, though, is ask for support from those you trust. And you'll usually be able to identify who those people are. They're the ones who don't offer judgments or specific advice but have the ability to simply listen to what you have to say, and to be there for you. Some friends may not know how to give you support; it may feel too scary for them because they sense that their parents are also vulnerable to infidelity; or perhaps it is too painful because they have "been there" themselves as children of infidelity and found it too upsetting, or have yet to resolve their own shameful feelings. Or maybe they simply don't know what to do to offer their emotional support. Some will keep their distance from you if they can't be helpful; others may act out—or blurt out insensitive remarks—leaving you feeling upset or ashamed.

Once Rachel realized why some of her friends may have spoken out as they had, she understood that when someone makes her feel ashamed of her father's infidelity, she needs to look at their remarks as a reflection of their own upbringing and unresolved issues rather than taking it personally. In a similar vein, when her parents' friends give her those judgmental "looks" that imply condemnation of her father's behavior or pity toward her for being his daughter, Rachel can tell herself that their reactions do not reflect who she, Rachel, actually is. She is not the person who engaged in "sleazy" behavior. She is, of course, closely connected to her father, but she is in no way responsible for or tainted by his mistakes.

As for Rachel's ongoing feelings of shame surrounding her father's behavior, she is now aware of how difficult it is for a child of any age to fully understand what is going on in his or her parents' intimate life. While Rachel and her sister were unintentionally affected by their father's affairs, they each have to realize how necessary it is for them to distance themselves emotionally from the crisis. The more they can do this, the more their sense of shame will lessen. It is my hope that Rachel's shameful feelings upon discovering that her father was less than the idealized person she had once thought him to be will ultimately give way to a more realistic understanding: there are no perfect human beings, and no perfect parents.

Zack's Story: "Moms are supposed to act like moms, not like some cheap whore."

Although Zack was only thirteen when he found out about his mother's affair, his reaction was not unlike Rachel's. In his case, however, he was also undergoing normal adolescent developmental changes, which contributed to his confusion and shame. Boys of twelve and thirteen are going through profound physical and emotional transitions. Before their eyes, they are slowly turning into men, and this dramatic shift baffles and excites them. Their voices strangely crack and deepen. They start to notice fuzz above their upper lip, as well as underarm and pubic hair. The signs of impending maturity make them feel both embarrassed and proud. Suddenly girls their age appear more mature and womanly, and feelings of attraction for the opposite sex (or the same sex if they are gay) begin to surface. Awkwardly unsure of themselves as soon-to-be sexual beings, they nonetheless are stimulated by the slightest sexual innuendo. It is a confusing yet exhilarating stage of development.

At a time when he was just beginning to cope with the dramatic changes of early adolescence, Zack was hit with the news of his mother's affair. Old enough to be aware of the potent force of sexual attraction but too young to understand adult relationships, he was shocked and angered by his mother's revelation. After being informed that she might be splitting up with Zack's father because she had met a man whom she cared for very much, Zack asked himself, "How could she be such a whore?" He said that thinking about his mom with another man "made me sick." What Zack was having a particularly hard time dealing with were the embarrassing comments and questions from his friends. He informed me that his pals would come out with such remarks as these: "Dude, who's the guy your mom is doing?" or, "Your mom must be pretty hot for her boyfriend to want to leave your dad," or, "How does your dad feel being shot down like that?" Zack said his mother had turned his life into "an X-rated movie," and he wondered how much more of it he could take.

Moms are supposed to act like moms, not like some cheap whore. I hated it that my friends thought of her that way. They wouldn't come right out and say it, but I could tell that's what they were thinking. And that's how I felt, too. I wanted her to be the way she was before the affair, so I wouldn't have to feel embarrassed about her anymore.

I didn't meet Zack until he was twenty-three, but had I known him at thirteen, I would have explained to him that parents sometimes act in ways that are unintentionally hurtful to their children, as well as terribly difficult for their children to understand. When Zack and I began our sessions, we talked about the fact that adolescence is a complicated time to confront a parent's infidelity, because one's own ideas about sexuality and intimate relationships are just beginning to form. Learning about your parent's affair when you are a teenager can often bring about such disturbing conditions as depression, anxiety, and panic attacks. And, as in Zack's case, feelings of shame and humiliation can cause a child of infidelity to withdraw from friends in an effort to protect himself from judgmental or salacious comments. Zack's sense of shame made him distance himself, not only from his male friends, but also from girls, whom he began to associate with qualities he perceived in his mother. He was easily angered by girls in school whose behavior seemed overly outgoing or flirtatious or, as Zack put it, "like a whore." He made disparaging remarks about such girls and put them down behind their backs, secretly wondering if all females were alike—untrustworthy and dishonorable.

In Zack's mind, his mother had fallen in love with this other man because he was wealthy. Part of his "proof" was that when she split up with his father and married the other man, his mom offered to buy Zack many of the material things he had always wanted: a guitar, a new cell phone, his own TV. He refused all of the proposed gifts because he thought that by accepting them, "I would have become just like her—prostituting myself." His mother wanted Zack to come and live with her, but he refused that offer as well. According to the teenage Zack, living with his mom and her new husband would have meant accepting her shameful betrayal.

It took Zack many years to finally accept that his mother was not a whore. After living an isolated life throughout high school, he began to make friends when he went away to college. In that new environment, he started to talk to young men who were involved in relationships and who discussed how difficult and complicated they were. At the same time, Zack realized that he longed for female company, which he had consciously rejected ever since he had felt so hurt and ashamed by his mother's affair. He developed a nonsexual relationship with a female friend, who became a trusted, nonjudgmental listener. Having opened up to her about his past, he realized that he wanted to start psychotherapy to better understand his feelings about his mother.

The first thing that Zack had to confront was his overriding tendency to be judgmental. He was very hard on the people around him and had a narrow concept of the "right way": his way. As he came to recognize this quality in himself, he challenged himself to be more open to how other people think and express themselves, how they behave, and what they expect from life. Zack realized that he was more rigid than he wanted to be and that he had probably learned to be this way from his father. With time, Zack was able to see his mother in a more objective light. He had always thought she was simply "too liberal," and he had never stopped to consider whether his assessment of her as a "whore" was actually valid. In fact, the only extramarital affair his mother had ever had was with the man who became her second husband, and with whom she had had a stable relationship ever since.

Ultimately, Zack was able to understand that his mother had felt restricted in her relationship with his father. His dad had reacted negatively to his mom's desire to begin a new career or start her own business, whereas her second husband encouraged her to lead a more fulfilling life. Although having an affair was not the best way to have resolved her marital problems, Zack's mom was not a whore. Zack recognized that throughout his teens and early twenties his thinking had been unbendingly black and white: good moms stay married to their husbands; bad moms are whores who betray their husbands and make their children feel ashamed.

Ten years after his life changed so drastically due to his mother's infidelity, Zack now realizes that had his parents been able to help him understand some of the reasons for his mom's affair, and had they given him the emotional support he so desperately needed back then, he might have felt less angry, less ashamed, and less isolated. Fortunately, Zack and his mother are finally able to talk about that major upheaval in both of their lives, and because the lines of communication are opening up, they look forward to a closer relationship.

WHAT IS SHAME—AND WHY DOES A PARENT'S INFIDELITY CAUSE IT?

Shame is part of a constellation of self-conscious emotions that include guilt, embarrassment, and pride. According to widely accepted psychological theory, shame is associated with the failure to live up to one's established standards of behavior. Children learn to set these standards primarily from their parents, who not only act as role models but also continually explain to their children about the right and wrong ways to act. Unfortunately, most parents use shame as a tool to teach their children correct behavior, even though shaming is a form of emotional abuse in that it stifles a child's developing self-esteem. A more positive approach would be to reinforce the attitudes, behaviors, and values that teach children right from wrong while also teaching them to think critically for themselves and make appropriate choices.

When children meet the standards set by their parents, they generally receive their parents' love and acceptance, and they also feel proud of themselves. When they fail to live up to those standards, they are usually made to feel ashamed of their actions by their parents' verbal condemnation or negative emotional response. Whereas guilt is associated with the focus on a specific wrongdoing, shame is associated with a condemnation of the self. In other words, when a child feels guilty, he focuses on why he shouldn't have done something in particular. When he feels ashamed, he focuses on what an unworthy or bad person he is. In certain dysfunctional families, parents use shaming in a highly abusive manner, making their children feel ashamed when they've done little or nothing to deserve either criticism or blame. Whether or not a child has acted in a way to deserve disapproval, shame makes him disapprove of himself.

So children learn that their unacceptable behavior—as defined largely by their parents—often causes their parents to disapprove of them, which in turn can cause them to feel ashamed. Feelings of having been ridiculed or humiliated stay with a child, and he learns to avoid those behaviors that would cause others to treat him in a humiliating manner. He tries to fit in with what is expected of him and do everything possible to comply with the established standards of behavior—first those of his parents and later on the standards of his peers—so that he can prevent feeling ashamed and instead feel accepted.

But what happens when the tables are turned? When the parent is the one whose behavior is unacceptable? When a parent "misbehaves" by having a sexual affair, the child nearly always disapproves of the behavior, but very often that child also ends up feeling ashamed—of his parent and himself.

Clients and survey respondents reported to me that the dishonorable behavior of the betraying parent as well as the ineffectual behavior of the betrayed parent (who was seemingly powerless to prevent the infidelity) damaged their own sense of self-esteem and caused them to feel ashamed. Children of infidelity thus not only felt ashamed of their parents, they felt ashamed of themselves. The following statements by adult children of infidelity reflect similar emotional consequences:

- "My parent's infidelity had a devastating effect on my self-esteem and self-respect. You see one or both parents disrespected and you start to wonder if you have done something to cause the affair."
- "I was at first very angry with my father for cheating. Once others became aware of the situation, I was also ashamed and embarrassed, as if his guilt was passed on to me."
- "I never told anybody about this. Never. Because in my head I thought, if I tell somebody, they're going to judge my family . . . When I thought about men who cheat on their wives, I thought, what a bunch of perverts—like pigs. And I didn't want anyone to think that about my family."
- "Deep down, I hated myself. It was this feeling that I was somehow a part of her [my mother's] deceptive, shabby treatment of my father. She was always so flirtatious and fake—why hadn't I been able to figure it all out?"

The last statement was made by a middle-aged woman named Marsha, who, when she was eleven years old, discovered letters that her mother had written to a friend describing an affair that would eventually break up her marriage to Marsha's father. When Marsha brought the letters to her mother asking what they meant, her mother slapped her across the face, saying, "You little twit! You know nothing about grown-up relationships. How dare you confront me!" Marsha was terrorized by her mother's reaction, as well as confused and angry about the affair. But she was also terribly ashamed of herself for having discovered the letters, for having gone to her mother with them, and for something that went much deeper. She told me that she felt dirty, as if the information she had unearthed about her mother was part of her own shameful self. Like many other children of infidelity,

Marsha felt ashamed of herself for her mother's behavior and felt the repercussions of that shame for many years. In Marsha's case, her mother intensified Marsha's sense of shame by making her feel that finding the letters was the act of wrongdoing, not the lies and betrayal inherent in the marital infidelity.

When one parent cheats on the other, a child of infidelity often feels that shame has been brought down upon the entire family. In the child's eyes, the betraying parent acted shamefully by lying to and cheating on the spouse; the betrayed parent bears the shame of being powerless to have prevented the infidelity; and the child feels ashamed for simply being part of a family that has been tainted by what she feels is immoral, embarrassing, or abhorrent behavior.

While parents may not be aware of it, when a child feels ashamed of her mother's or father's infidelity, the experience can diminish her own self-esteem. A child perceives that her parent is not the person he or she had always been; that she, the child, is somehow connected to the wrongdoing; and regardless of her age, she feels open to ridicule and feelings of degradation. In other words, she feels bad about herself—and ashamed of herself.

We have all experienced shame at some point in our lives, because it is usually the way we have been socialized to do the right thing. Consequently, most of us are very concerned about how we are perceived by others, and we do what we can to prevent feeling ashamed of ourselves. When one or both parents do something fundamentally wrong, such as cheating on the other spouse, which the family, the child, and society consider to be a demeaning of core values, a child's moral structure collapses, and shame takes hold.

I FEEL GUILTY FOR TELLING ON MY PARENT/ I FEEL GUILTY FOR KEEPING THE SECRET

As we noted earlier, shame and guilt are closely related. In the course of my research for this book, I heard from numerous children and adult children who talked about how guilty they felt for either "telling on" their unfaithful parent or withholding incriminating information from their betrayed parent. Sadly, many children of infidelity are either intentionally or unintentionally forced to play a role in their parent's adultery scenario by keeping or divulging the secret that one parent is cheating on the other, and this can't help but bring about feelings of guilt. An adulterous parent whose child inadvertently discovers "the secret" may enlist that child's support by advising him to "let this be our little secret" or telling him not to tell the other parent because "it would hurt Mom (or Dad) too much." Of course, a child—regardless of his age—is in a no-win situation. If he keeps the secret, he will feel guilty for withholding devastating information from the betrayed parent. If he divulges the secret, he will feel guilty for causing the betrayed parent to become terribly upset, for possibly causing his parents to split up, and for betraying the trust of the unfaithful parent.

The following survey respondents' comments were typical of many I have heard from clients and others who bore the guilt of either keeping or divulging their parent's infidelity secret:

- "I was my mother's 'special friend' because I kept her secrets of infidelity without realizing it. [Eventually] it was I who told my father about her affair, as she attempted to lie to him about where we had been, and I corrected her. I was eight years old. My father left shortly after and never came back except to visit after a couple of years went by. My mother blamed me and said it was my fault, and in a way it was."

• "I was so young, I didn't quite understand what was going on, but I knew it wasn't right. I told on my mom, and my dad beat her for it. She held a grudge for years, but it was never spoken. I became my dad's favorite child after that."

• "I didn't like having to keep the secret of my mother's affair from my father. Even as a kid, I was open-minded, but I had a strong moral understanding. And any kind of lie felt wrong. So I didn't like being part of the lie."

In the following scenario, Pamela reveals how she was forced to harbor "dark secrets" to demonstrate "respect" for her unfaithful father. It is my sense that keeping such information under wraps for so long must have made Pamela feel terribly conflicted about her role in her parents' relationship and guilty for the unsolicited part she had to play.

The last act of infidelity before the divorce was but one in a series of what appeared to be extramarital affairs. Women who refused to identify themselves would call the house asking for my father during the hours when my mother was not yet home from work but I was home from school. Because I realized something was amiss, I never shared with my mother the fact that these women were calling, and in the end, I felt as though I was harboring dark secrets for my father, though I'm not certain he ever realized that it had that effect on me.

In the end, I felt as though my father was counting on the silence of his children (I'm sure I wasn't the only one who had a hunch that things were amiss; my older sisters probably knew more than I did) so that he could continue doing what he was doing without ever having to be accountable to his family for the poor choices he was making. I'm almost certain that because we were raised in a very traditional household where the father reigns supreme that he knew full well none of his daughters would ever speak a word about what he was doing, because to do so would have been akin to disrespecting him.

Ellen is another child of infidelity who was put in the position of having to hide her unfaithful parent's secret. She was twelve when she noticed that her mother always seemed to go out with a certain male friend when Ellen's father was out of town on business. Ellen didn't really know what was going on between her mom and the man until the man started bringing his son to the house to hang out with Ellen. At that point, Ellen says she began to "put two and two together."

I think what my mother and that man thought was that by getting me and the son to be friends, it would divert attention from the two of them and what they were doing. They thought that if I became friends with the son, it would be an excuse for them to be together. But one time when this man brought his son over to hang out with me and my friends, I got suspicious and went to look for my mom and the man, and I couldn't find them anywhere in the house. I guess they had gone back to his place or whatever.

I didn't say anything, and I think my dad might have known something was going on, but he never said anything either. But a few months later, my father came home from a trip early and my mom had told me she was at the mall. He kept asking me, "Where is she at, who is she with? You must know . . . and you're not going to tell me?" Apparently my dad had found some cards from this man to my mom. I didn't want to lie to him, so I just kept saying, "He's just a friend, dad, he's just a friend." But he showed me the cards and said, "Do you think these are from someone who is just a friend?"

The hardest part for me was that I felt used and dirty. My mom had brought this man to our house and disrespected it. And it made me feel worse that she used this man's son to silence me. I don't ever remember her saying "Don't tell your dad"—I just didn't. And people in the family knew and didn't say anything. So I felt dirty and ashamed.

If children are put in the position of having to choose who to be loyal to when one parent cheats, they inadvertently become an accomplice to one or the other parent. If they divulge the secret, they are betraying the unfaithful parent, and they will likely feel guilty about the dire consequences. The information they bring to light will probably cause the betrayed parent to feel angry and distraught— and may even cause the marriage to end. Feeling responsible for such high-stakes consequences is an extremely painful burden. By keeping the secret, however, a child is siding with the unfaithful parent and thus becomes a betrayer herself, which usually breeds an intense sense of guilt. And, as Ellen disclosed, keeping the secret can also make a child feel that she is tainted by the unsavory behavior of her betraying parent, linked to the parent's sexual betrayal, and made to feel "dirty and ashamed." So whichever choice she makes, the child confronted with keeping or revealing her parent's infidelity secret has no safe options. She will feel guilty and torn either way, as the "right thing to do" becomes overshadowed by a shameful choice between betraying one parent or the other.

Many respondents in our survey had to face such a no-win decision, because the betraying parent demanded that they "keep the secret"—and that they thus participate in the machinations of the extramarital affair. When a child is asked to become a co-conspirator in this way, he or she learns at a young age what it means to betray someone you love. Sadly, being forced to make the choice between betraying your cheating parent or your betrayed parent is a traumatic event that will most likely create lasting emotional scars.

I'M ASHAMED OF MY PARENT'S HYPOCRISY

Because parents are their children's primary teachers of morality, children are particularly sensitive to any perceived evidence that a parent might be saying one thing and doing another. This goes for six-year-olds as well as sixteen- or twenty-six-year-olds. "I thought you said sugar wasn't good for me," a first-grader might ask his mom, "so why is daddy allowed to eat so much candy?" Or a teenager might want to know why he can't experiment with marijuana when he knows for a fact that you did when you were his age.

How does the "practice what you preach" dilemma relate to parents who cheat? I heard from a number of children of infidelity whose sense of shame was based on their parent having preached a particular set of values only to then demonstrate their own flagrant disregard for those values. The son's or daughter's feeling was that they were particularly ashamed to be associated with a parent who was a hypocrite, because hypocrisy was worse than simply doing the wrong thing. Here are some representative excerpts from survey respondents:

- "My father was always very righteous and demanding about me doing the right thing. It was very disappointing finding out that the person who always demanded good values from me betrayed his own values." (Male in his thirties)
- "My father was an extremely religious man in a very unforgiving and rigid way. I saw him be very judgmental of people who cheated. To find out he had cheated was a real blow." (Female in her fifties)
- "The infidelity was hurtful not only because of the act itself but also because of what it signified: lack of respect for my mother, lack of consideration for the family unit, and the act itself was

contrary to the way we had been raised—to be respectful, strong, and committed to the decisions/choices we make in life." (Female in her thirties)

- "When I was fourteen, my mother forbade me from wearing a two-piece bathing suit because she thought it was too sexy. It was similar to what all the girls my age were wearing, but she had a fit that I had bought it. Meanwhile, she was not only wearing tight skirts and low-cut blouses, she was having an affair that broke up her marriage to my father." (Female in her forties)

- "Shortly before my sister and I found out that my dad had been cheating on my mom, he made it a point to forbid me from going over to my sister's apartment because it was 'a house of sin.' I was seventeen and my sister was twenty. What he meant was that my sister was living with her boyfriend, and this was back when living together wasn't as accepted as it is now. When we found out about his affairs, I couldn't believe what a hypocrite he was! Isn't living with your boyfriend less sinful than cheating on your wife?" (Female in her fifties)

- "My father was very conservative and had very strict morals. He went to church every week. When I was in my early twenties, I found out he had a lover. I lost all respect for him, because he had always taught us the opposite of how he was now acting. I was very disappointed in him, and we became very distant." (Male in his thirties)

Having been brought up to respect the values their parents espoused, children of infidelity are affronted by their parents' hypocrisy and feel shame on their behalf. It's as if the tables are turned, and the child or adult child is forced to mentally say to the offending parent, "Shame on you. You have broken the rules." But parents don't usually intend to break the rules. They most often have the best of intentions when it comes to teaching their children morals and values and being good examples of those values. For some, their professed values are derived from religious principles; for others, they may reflect a more secular philosophy of life. In either case, when a parent's personal needs or desires cause them to contradict the values they have taught their children, they are perceived as teaching one way of life and living another. Children are left thinking, "What hypocrites my parents are!" It's as if their cheating parent is saying, "These are the values I want you to adhere to, but I am not able to follow them myself." Parents who previously guided, advised, and helped a child solve moral conflicts may now feel disabled by the infidelity drama and unable to provide moral guidance. And yet, a child needs to know that his parents are doing something to address the issue of "saying one thing and doing another."

So what can a parent whose child feels ashamed of him or her do to explain why people are often unable to stick to their moral values? The following guidelines may help.

HOW PARENTS CAN HELP CHILDREN OF INFIDELITY DEAL WITH FEELINGS OF SHAME

1. **Respectfully confront your child's feelings of shame.** Just as it's not enough for the cheating parent to offer a quick "I'm sorry; please forgive me" and hope that the crisis will be over, it's also not enough to simply insist that a child "need not feel ashamed." When we try to get by with such quick fixes, we're denying the impact parental infidelity has on a child and denying his feelings about it. Families need to take the time to process the intense feelings concerning what took place. You might tell your child some-

thing like this: "I understand that you feel ashamed (of me/of your mother/of your father), and you have the right to feel that way. However, the most important thing is for you to know that I (or the other parent) brought about the shame that you are feeling, and I (or he/she) am going to learn from my mistake, because I don't want to feel ashamed of myself—and I don't want you to feel ashamed of me either. But remember, you did nothing to bring about the shameful feelings you are experiencing."

2. **Let your child know that the problems between you and your spouse are not his fault—and show him that you love him.** A child who feels guilty or ashamed about one parent cheating on the other needs you to show him that you love him regardless of what is going on between you and your spouse.

3. **Never expect your child to lie to or betray the other parent.** Forcing a child to do so causes a painful sense of guilt and shame. Don't turn your child into the scapegoat for your infidelity crisis.

4. **Help children understand that even painful life experiences— such as feeling ashamed of your parents—can offer life lessons.** When parents act in unexpected or disappointing ways, it can offer a challenging, albeit difficult, learning experience for children. Although it can be crushing for a child of any age to witness his parent's failure to live up to professed moral values, the crisis of infidelity can yield important life lessons. Among them, a young child learns that "Even grown-ups make serious mistakes" and an older child discovers that "My parents have flaws and may not always be able to live up to their own moral standards."

HOW ADULT CHILDREN OF INFIDELITY CAN DEAL WITH FEELINGS OF SHAME

Many of the above guidelines can apply to your own process of healing from the shame of parental infidelity. Review them and use those that seem applicable.

Shame can serve as an inner guide to help us create the kind of life we want for ourselves. For instance, if there is a choice you face that involves a moral decision, one in which you ask yourself, "Should I or shouldn't I?" you can look back to your experience of parental infidelity and consider this question: "Given what I learned then, would I feel ashamed of myself if I go in this direction?" Understanding why we feel ashamed can provide us with a reflection of what we truly value in life—and how we can balance our needs and desires with our treatment of those we love. As an adult child of infidelity, the crisis you experienced growing up can offer you the opportunity to reexamine your own values, expand your awareness of human behavior and frailties, and reset your own moral compass.

READER/CUSTOMER CARE SURVEY

HEFG

We care about your opinions! Please take a moment to fill out our online Reader Survey at **http://survey.hcibooks.com**.
As a **"THANK YOU"** you will receive a **VALUABLE INSTANT COUPON** towards future book purchases
as well as a **SPECIAL GIFT** available only online! Or, you may mail this card back to us.

(PLEASE PRINT IN ALL CAPS)

First Name _____ MI. ____ Last Name _____

Address _____ City _____

State ____ Zip ____ Email _____

1. Gender
☐ Female ☐ Male

2. Age
☐ 8 or younger ☐ 13-16
☐ 9-12 ☐ 21-30
☐ 17-20 ☐ 31+

3. Did you receive this book as a gift?
☐ Yes ☐ No

4. Annual Household Income
☐ under $25,000
☐ $25,000 - $34,999
☐ $35,000 - $49,999
☐ $50,000 - $74,999
☐ over $75,000

5. What are the ages of the children living in your house?
☐ 0 - 14 ☐ 15+

6. Marital Status
☐ Single
☐ Married
☐ Divorced
☐ Widowed

7. How did you find out about the book?
(please choose one)
☐ Recommendation
☐ Store Display
☐ Online
☐ Catalog/Mailing
☐ Interview/Review

8. Where do you usually buy books?
(please choose one)
☐ Bookstore
☐ Online
☐ Book Club/Mail Order
☐ Price Club (Sam's Club, Costco's, etc.)
☐ Retail Store (Target, Wal-Mart, etc.)

9. What subject do you enjoy reading about the most?
(please choose one)
☐ Parenting/Family
☐ Relationships
☐ Recovery/Addictions
☐ Health/Nutrition

☐ Christianity
☐ Spirituality/Inspiration
☐ Business Self-help
☐ Women's Issues
☐ Sports

10. What attracts you most to a book?
(please choose one)
☐ Title
☐ Cover Design
☐ Author
☐ Content

TAPE IN MIDDLE; DO NOT STAPLE

BUSINESS REPLY MAIL
FIRST-CLASS MAIL PERMIT NO 45 DEERFIELD BEACH, FL

POSTAGE WILL BE PAID BY ADDRESSEE

Health Communications, Inc.
3201 SW 15th Street
Deerfield Beach FL 33442-9875

FOLD HERE

Comments

FOUR

What Does Marriage Mean if My Parents Cheat but Stay Together?

Throughout our lives, my dad would meet these "really nice ladies"—that's what he would call them—"Oh, so and so is a really nice lady," which was the code for "I'm sleeping with her" or "I'm going to sleep with her." So when he used that code, my sisters and I would know something was going on. And then my mother would be really jealous and little arguments would start over things like, "Why did you park the car the wrong way?" or "Why did you forget the bread at the store?" She couldn't come right out and say, "Hey, you're having an affair with somebody, aren't you?"

But they never got divorced. My mom loved my dad, but she also needed him to survive economically. My dad loved my mom, but he didn't love love her—he tolerated her.

—*Nick, thirty-nine*

How can she be so blind? My mom is just kidding herself.
She thinks my dad is going to change into a husband who
won't cheat. How can she stay married to him?

—*Katie, fifteen*

Some couples find that their marriages become stronger once they deal with the underlying issues that caused marital infidelity. When this is the case, their children can benefit by witnessing the effort parents make to repair the marriage. Other couples realize the relationship can't be repaired, so they get divorced. Although adapting to divorce is often very painful for children, at least the situation is clear-cut: Mom and Dad can't get along so they're splitting up. But what effect does it have on a child when one parent accepts the other's unfaithfulness as a fact of life or something to put up with for the sake of the family? When one or both parents continue to stay together and cheat, what message does it send to children about the meaning of love, intimacy, and marriage? How do children deal with the confusion they feel when their parents stay married despite continued episodes of adultery?

In this chapter, we'll discuss the various reasons why unfaithful and betrayed partners make the decision to stay in their marriage, and how each of these reasons can have a particular impact on children. We'll hear from those whose parents stayed together despite ongoing infidelity, and how this affected their childhood and their relationships as adults. I'll offer advice to parents as well as adult children of infidelity who are dealing with the particular pain and confusion that can result when unfaithful partners stay married to each other.

First, let's consider the reasons parents in an unfaithful marriage decide to stay together.

WHY DO THEY STAY TOGETHER?

Fifty-eight percent of our survey respondents told us that their parents stayed married even though one or both was unfaithful. Like Nick, some respondents revealed that a parent was unfaithful throughout the marriage, leaving the son or daughter to feel cynical and confused about what marriage really means. Given that divorce has grown more prevalent and is considered less of a social taboo, and with surveys showing that most people believe faithfulness is the most important prerequisite for a successful marriage, why do so many people in unfaithful marriages decide to stay the course? There are a number of reasons why such couples don't divorce, each of which can have a specific effect on a child.

Some couples stay together for the sake of the children, perhaps believing that an imperfect or even hostile relationship between parents is less detrimental to a child than living between two households. Depending on the particular circumstances, this may or may not be true. If an unfaithful spouse makes the choice to be monogamous from that point forward, if the betrayed spouse can get past the resentment, and if both partners come to an understanding about why one was unfaithful to the other, the marriage could very well improve and become stronger. In such cases, children would clearly benefit from living in an intact home in which the parents were reconnected and loving.

But what if the infidelity is ongoing? Some betrayed spouses may have the ability to accept their partner's infidelity without feeling resentful or bitter, although I believe such individuals are extremely rare. What usually happens is that a betrayed spouse's resentment and rage fester as the cheating spouse continues to be unfaithful. If the marriage is held together solely by the belief in staying married for the sake of the children, and those children witness their parents being unloving, unfaithful, and hostile toward each other, the message kids likely come away with is: marriage is a loveless, painful charade.

There are other cases in which an affair, or even a series of affairs, may be perceived as a temporary situation that can be resolved. Couples may believe that infidelity on the part of one or both spouses is evidence of problems in the marriage that can be worked out. For many couples this may be true; with time and concerted effort, the marriage may improve, and if it does, that can't help but benefit the children as well. For other couples, things do not work out, yet they stay together anyway. One or both partners may continue to have affairs, thereby perpetuating the cycle of secrets, lies, and betrayal, which will almost certainly affect children in a negative way.

Sometimes a betrayed parent might feel that infidelity is just a stage that the unfaithful parent will outgrow. Perhaps such individuals believe that their spouse needed to get the thrill of an extramarital affair out of his or her system, and that from now on they'll be able to commit themselves to a monogamous marriage. But if the cheating parent doesn't intend to be monogamous, how might the betrayed parent's unrealistic belief affect the children? If younger children are told something along the lines that Mommy or Daddy "made a mistake but is not going to make that mistake again," it may set them up for more disappointment if the infidelity continues. And older children like Katie, whose comments appear above, may view their betrayed yet hopeful parent as unable to face reality. Such kids may lose respect for both parents and become cynical about the possibility of married love.

Then there are those men and women who believe that "it's a fact of life that men have affairs—but it's not a reason to divorce." This belief is especially true in certain cultures, where male infidelity is not only accepted but expected. It's no surprise that the lesson this belief teaches children is that "Even though women don't like it, it's okay for men to be unfaithful." Interestingly, although many of our survey respondents come from cultures that adhere to this belief, they still reported being hurt by their father's unfaithfulness, and their own adult relationships still reflected the various deleterious reactions we are exploring in this book.

Another reason spouses may remain in a marriage when one or both are unfaithful is that both partners might believe that monogamy is merely an ideal, whereas infidelity is the reality. (This is not the same as a so-called "open marriage" in which extramarital relationships are accepted or encouraged by both partners and are not kept secret. Presumably, children in such marriages are informed of this arrangement.) This is similar to the "It's a fact of life that men have affairs" reason, except that women are included in the projected expectation of adultery. When parents rationalize infidelity in this manner, it can lead children to become cynical early on and to expect infidelity in their own future relationships.

Then there are those couples who stay married even when infidelity is ongoing because one or both partners may not be emotionally ready to disengage from the marriage, perhaps due to anxiety or depression, dependence or codependence, or even a childhood trauma. Children in such marriages are left to conclude that parents are powerless to change an unhappy situation and that marriage is a relationship in which you can become sadly confined.

Financial considerations are another reason why some partners in unfaithful marriages choose to stay together. A betrayed partner might put up with infidelity because it may seem impossible to make it on his or her own, or because an unfaithful spouse is preferable to a diminished material lifestyle. In such cases, children receive the message that marriage is essentially about practical considerations, rather than love and trust.

Finally, some couples eschew divorce for religious reasons. While adultery may be considered a sin, divorce is strictly forbidden in some religions. When parents in an unfaithful marriage stay together due to religious beliefs, children may be left feeling skeptical about both marriage and religious practice.

In Nick's case, his mother never considered divorcing her unfaithful husband because, as much pain as his affairs caused her, she continued to love him—and need him. And although Nick's father continuously felt the need to "roam," he also felt an obligation to the family. Unfortunately, neither his mother's enduring love for his father nor his father's sense of familial obligation prevented Nick from suffering the repercussions of parental infidelity.

Nick's Story: "The more my father had affairs, the more my mom held on to him."

Nick was a young boy when he first became aware of his dad talking about a "nice lady" he had just met. He was the youngest of four and the only boy, and while his sisters knew about their father's affairs, initially Nick knew only that his parents fought a lot and that his mother often pleaded with his father not to go out, to stay home with her and the family. It would take a while for Nick to understand that his father's reference to "a nice lady" was the code phrase meaning that he was sleeping with a new woman.

Nick describes his parents' relationship as "filled with drama...a lot of yelling and screaming and crying, and 'please don't go'—that kind of stuff." Although his mother refrained from directly confronting her husband about the affairs, she was often terribly upset by the long stretches he spent away from home. Instead of accusing him of infidelity, she would pick fights with Nick's father about seemingly insignificant domestic issues. As Nick recalls, "There were always these little nitpicky things that would really have a lot of venom behind them on both sides. So there would be really weird arguments that we kids would take notice of." Nick remembers a period of time when his dad lived in an adjacent town during the week—about two hours away—to secure work. As Nick got older, he realized that his father was using his out-of-town residence as a place to invite women. His sisters and mother were aware of this arrangement as well; nevertheless, on the weekends, the whole family greeted Nick's dad with open arms.

When he came home on the weekends and brought his paycheck, we were all happy to see him, and my mom was happy to see him, too. But we also knew that it hurt her to know that he was probably having affairs during the week and meeting these "really nice ladies" and stuff like that. So that always really hurt. I loved my mom very much. She was my source of unconditional love, and to see somebody hurt, somebody you love, it's a scary thing.

Sometimes she would go through these manic phases where she'd say things like, "We're gonna pack up and leave, and when he comes back this weekend, we're gonna be gone," but then she'd say, "We can't live without him; what are we gonna do if he leaves?" When things got really bad, she would send us off to our aunt's house, and then sometimes when I'd come back from staying with my aunt, I'd come in and see that furniture had been broken or was missing. I could tell that there had been fights. Not physical fights between them, but my mom was so angry that her love turned to rage and she would break things. So that was always really confusing as a kid to come home and find that the brass tray on the coffee table was missing. Or figurines were broken.

When I asked Nick why he thought his parents stayed together, he began his explanation by telling me the history of their relationship. They had married when they were both teenagers, and each had looked at marriage as a way to escape their families. Nick's mother had been in love with Nick's father from the beginning, but for Nick's father, his heart was never completely given over to his wife.

My mother loved my dad, and my dad kind of liked my mom, but [before they got married] he was really in love with somebody else who wouldn't give him the time of day. So that was already a mistake right there. I guess in his mind, he settled for somebody who loved him, but he always had this thing that, "there's somebody out there who's better," the grass is always greener. He always had this wanderlust that he had to be free and roam. It's strange and it's sad. And I guess if all this had happened today, we would see him as a sex addict.

So the more he had affairs, the more my mom would hold on to him. It made him miserable, and it made her miserable, but it kept him there. It kept them both in a miserable relationship that they shouldn't have ever gotten into in the first place. She was so in love with him. But the more she would hold on to him, the more he would feel, "I have to leave; I have to move." I think he stayed because, even though he had this need to look for other women, he wasn't strong enough to be his own man. And he felt that he had an obligation to the family. This was back in the sixties and seventies when women still couldn't really support a family on their own. And my mother was uneducated, left school when she got married. He was the breadwinner in the family.

So Nick's father stayed in the marriage primarily out of a sense of obligation, while his mother resented the affairs but still loved her husband—and needed to stay married to him to survive economically. It's interesting that Nick's sense of confusion and fear as a child—confusion about the meaning of love and marriage and fear that his father would leave forever—translated into a pattern of clinging to and running from his love relationships as an adult. Nick is gay, and he would like to be in a stable, committed relationship, but he has had a difficult time undoing the emotional proclivities he inherited from each of his parents. He told me that he identifies with his mother's insecurity as well as his father's desire to be unencumbered and free. In his own adult relationships, Nick has pleaded with lovers not to leave him, but he has also been the one to cut off relationships even when things were going well. He recognizes that his behavior reflects both his mother's fear of losing her husband and his father's long-held yearning to "roam."

> *The more my father had affairs or showed attention to other women, the more my mother would hold on to him. When you're a child, and that's the model for a relationship, your [future] relationships are already flawed to begin with. [As an adult], you fall into that pattern because it's what you know. . . . There's a part of me that when I'm in a relationship, I emulate that part of my mother that I want to hold on to somebody and just flood them with really intense emotions to show them how much I care about them. But then I also have this part of me that's like my dad, which is: "Maybe there's something more on the other side of the fence; maybe I'm settling; maybe this person isn't the right one for me"; or maybe I just want to go out and have sex with somebody even though I'm in a committed relationship. So I've got these two parts of me that are conflicted.*

Nick's comments are evidence that he has become exceedingly self-aware as an adult. He knows he has to overcome some difficult emotional obstacles before he can enjoy a healthy relationship, and he is able to pinpoint where some of those obstacles originated. Over the course of our interview, he let me know that he felt very close to his mother both as a young boy and later in his life as well. He empathized with the anguish she endured due to his father's constant unfaithfulness and was clear in his condemnation of infidelity as a painful wedge between husband and wife, father and child.

And yet, Nick was also forthcoming about the affairs he has had with married men. It is this aspect of his behavior that he says he finds particularly "despicable," but he also says he is baffled as to why he engaged in the very behavior that once made his mother so miserable.

> *It scares me to admit that I'm like my dad, that I sabotage my relationships, and that I want to cheat on my partner. What's even more despicable is that I've even had sex with married men. So I don't know where that came from; I don't know why that happens. But looking back on it, I'm not really proud [of my behavior]. That's really acting on impulse, like my dad. Maybe it's sex addiction. I don't know, but it's troubling to know that I've acted in that way. And then also to know that these guys [who I've slept with] are married with wives and kids—that they would have sex with another guy.*

Nick seems to feel scornful not only of himself but of the married men with whom he's had affairs—because they have wives and kids. When he had affairs with married men, he identified with his own father but also with his lover's wife and children. He knew how they would have felt if they had found out about the affair, because he had experienced such feelings as a child. It was particularly relevant that Nick had the affairs with married men after his mother died. He told me that he had a very difficult and lengthy time grieving her death, and while he considered the sexual liaisons to be devoid of real emotion, he has had second thoughts about the meaning of those brief relationships:

> *When my mother died, I really just shut my emotions off to the whole world. . . . Finally, when I did start to come back to life again, I hadn't been dating anybody and hadn't been sexually active, so I kind of just needed to be around people. And be around men, I guess. So I met some married guys, and we would have sex, and there was no emotion involved. And then when it was over, I felt bad. I felt, Why did I do that? That's somebody's husband, that's somebody's father . . . I didn't feel like having a relationship with anybody, because I didn't want to risk having emotions with somebody who might go away or die or something like that. And during that whole time, of course I still hated my dad. I hated my dad for treating my mom so awful and cheating on her. Meanwhile, I was having sex with married men.*

After telling me that he hadn't been ready for emotional involvement following his mother's death, but that he had had affairs with married men, he added, "But I still needed to be intimate with somebody, and to me intimacy is sex." So there was some confusion in Nick's mind about the link between emotional involvement, intimacy, and sex—as there must have been confusion in his mind when he was a child looking at his parents' marriage. His mother wanted emotional and sexual intimacy with her husband, who wasn't providing it but was sexually intimate with other women. As an adult, Nick has been left with a sense of fear and yearning when approaching both emotional and sexual intimacy.

In his attempts to become intimate with the men he has been involved with, Nick alternately has played the role of his "roaming" father, his desperate mother, and the lover who threatens the stability of another person's marriage. It was as if he was trying to piece together a relationship from the fragmented portrait of a marriage that he had witnessed as a child. Playing these three roles, he sought to discover what love is really about. Confused about the nature of love and intimacy due to his parents' torn, chaotic relationship, Nick tried to get close to someone through sex but at the same time shut himself off from developing an intimate connection.

You cannot force yourself to be intimate, nor can you impose intimacy on someone else; it is something that can develop only when you allow yourself to be vulnerable. Nick tried to force himself to be intimate, but he wasn't ready; he was still protecting himself from the type of pain he felt as a child whose household included sexual betrayal, resentment, and sadness. Nick will need to resolve those infidelity-related issues before he can become truly open to receiving and giving love. Only then can an authentically loving connection develop with someone who is also available for intimacy.

WHEN UNFAITHFUL PARENTS STAY TOGETHER, HOW DO CHILDREN FEEL?

Children and adult children of infidelity may react in a variety of ways to their parents' decision to stay together despite ongoing unfaithfulness. With betrayal, accusations, secrets, lies, anger, and sadness a constant in their home, children may have one or more of the following responses (italicized excerpts are from survey respondents):

Angry Because Parents Don't Face Their Problems

"I feel angry at my father [who has Internet sex] because he will not go to counseling to help their marriage."

Although even young children may accept that their parents have problems, they expect them to be able to solve them. Not yet aware of the fact that some adults can't always face their troubles, younger children may get angry when they witness their parents fighting or constantly being upset. Older children, like the respondent above, may feel angry when parents appear to be ignoring the problem of unfaithful behavior. As we have suggested earlier, adult children of infidelity benefit when they can develop an awareness that parents are human beings with flaws, one of which may be the inability to confront serious personal issues. It is a challenge to come to that awareness because it requires objectivity, which is not an easy perspective to have when a child of infidelity is filled with anger over his parents' inability to deal with ongoing lies and hurtful behavior. The bottom line is that when parents are unable to resolve their problems, children of any age are left with a sense of insecurity and disappointment, which often manifests as anger.

Intolerant of Parents' Hostility and Indecisiveness

"I have an incredibly difficult time talking to either of my parents when they start degrading each other because I think they had the option of changing their relationship status. I'm incredibly intolerant of indecision or inconsistency in relationships."

"I have spent my life listening to recriminations between the two, but in the end they never decided to take the final step and divorce."

Children of infidelity need to realize that not making a decision to separate and divorce is a decision in itself. It is a choice to continue in the marriage even though the couple has serious problems. The above respondents have to accept that their parents have decided that, despite the infidelity, recriminations, and degrading treatment of each other, this is the lifestyle that the couple is willing to put up with. Otherwise, they would have made another decision. Or maybe they are not yet ready to make the decision to split up—or to go to counseling to improve the relationship. Perhaps they will head in that direction later, when they are ready. Or maybe they will never feel ready. Not everyone can face divorce or separation, even when their relationship is causing them a great deal of pain.

The decision to break up a marriage is a traumatic one, and it is often complicated by cultural, religious, or family messages advising against divorce. So it is rarely an easy decision to make. Very often children of infidelity believe that parents should take action one way or another—either get divorced or resolve their problems—and they are confused by their parents' seeming inability to do so. But nobody knows other than the parents themselves when they are ready for whatever action should be taken.

Puzzled by the Betrayed Parent's Tolerance of Her/His Spouse's Infidelity

"My father has cheated on my mother since the beginning of their relationship and still does to this day, thirty-five years later. I can't understand why she continues to tolerate it."

Sometimes there are cultural reasons why women tolerate male infidelity. In more male-dominant cultures, men are given implicit permission to have extramarital affairs, and women often feel they have no choice but to accept their husband's unfaithfulness. The above respondent wonders why her mother has tolerated thirty-five years of cheating. Maybe it's because her mother feels she has no other options or because she is dependent on her husband economically and has been more concerned with the welfare of her children than her own happiness. Or perhaps this woman comes from a family in which there were infidelity issues between her own parents, so that putting up with an unfaithful husband feels familiar to her. Maybe she was raised without a father and therefore wanted to make sure that her own children had a father in the home, even if it has meant sacrificing her own self-esteem. Although all of these reasons for putting up with an unfaithful marriage make a certain kind of sense, the respondent's mother may not realize that by tolerating her husband's adultery for thirty-five years, she has provided her children with two unfortunate role models: male infidelity and female acceptance of it.

Resentful of Being Forced to Mediate Between Belligerent Parents

"Very often I'm made the mediator because they don't talk to each other."

It is terribly unfair and unhealthy to impose the role of mediator on a child of infidelity. The need for a third person to help the parents communicate and resolve their problems may be very real, but that person needs to be an objective professional, not the couple's child or adult child. When a child is forced to become part of a triangulated relationship with her parents, she is implicated in their resentments, accusations, and battles. In addition to suffering from her own anger, disappointment, sadness, and insecurity surrounding her parents' infidelity scenario, she is thrown into the center of their traumatic crisis.

Then there is the possibility that a child may achieve a degree of success in mediating between her parents. When this is the case, she will probably feel a sense of omnipotence because she has proven herself capable of fixing the most crucial problem in her life—the fractured relationship between her parents. This success can give a child of any age a sense of empowerment, but it also sets up unrealistic expectations. The next time her parents need her to "fix" the problems between them, how will she react when she is unable to do so? Chances are she will feel a sense of frustration, worthlessness, and guilt. She may feel as if she is not smart enough or good enough to repair her parents' troubled relationship, and she will thus feel disempowered. Because her efforts in this important cause were not fruitful, more than likely the experience will stand out as a significant failure in her life. When confronted with future crises, this failure may resonate and deprive her of the confidence she needs.

Playing the mediator between two parents in an unfaithful marriage is never an appropriate role for a child, regardless of their age. It is actually a healthy sign that the above respondent is resentful of being placed in this position; it means that she is aware of the inappropriateness of her parents' demands.

Sympathetic When a Betrayed Parent Retaliates with Infidelity

"When my mother finally found out about my father's infidelity, and since my father had been so inattentive over the years, she, too, had an affair. . . . I didn't fault her for doing it because my father has never really loved my mother. I felt sorry for her. She was always so lonely. I could see why she was driven to commit adultery."

Although it is understandable for a child to sympathize with a betrayed parent, feeling sympathetic toward a parent's retaliatory infidelity doesn't really make sense, because when a spouse who has been sexually betrayed retaliates by cheating, he or she is merely punishing the other person—and punishment doesn't resolve whatever issues underlie an unfaithful marriage. Rather, it complicates the relationship even more. Now there are two people keeping secrets from each other, two people hurting each other, and two people betraying their family's trust. Moreover, children of infidelity are thus taught that the best way to deal with someone who hurts you is to get even by hurting them back.

Confused by the "Mixed Messages" Sent by One or Both Parents

"She constantly cried to me about her suspicions, telling me my father must be spending time with one of his girlfriends and that she couldn't stand to be with a man who cheats. And yet in the next breath, she would ask me how she could ever live without him. That she loved him. It was crazy-making."

Indeed, it can be crazy-making for a child of infidelity to be on the receiving end of a parent's mixed messages. A betrayed parent might talk about the cheating parent's redeeming qualities or become nostalgic for the "good times" before adultery was discovered. And then in the next breath, he or she may go into a tirade against the spouse's deceitful heartlessness. At times, the cheating parent might blame the betrayed parent for having caused the need to stray; then, at other times, plead for forgiveness. Such conflicting feelings can certainly be tough for a daughter or son to comprehend. Like the above respondent, a child of infidelity wonders how her parent can possibly love someone who is making her so miserable. Another child might wonder how a cheating spouse can blame his wife in one breath and then condemn himself in the next.

But such contradictions are part of being human. Feeling rage toward a spouse for their sexual betrayal doesn't necessarily erase one's feelings of tenderness toward that person, which makes it that much more difficult to decide which course the relationship should take. Getting help from a psychologist or marriage counselor can help couples sort out their complex feelings and make beneficial decisions about the relationship, but frequently this route is avoided. Instead, parents in an unfaithful marriage often stay together and continue to send mixed messages—and children continue to feel upset, frustrated, and confused.

Whether a child of infidelity reacts with intolerance, anger, resentment, sympathy, or a mix of emotions, when parents make the decision to stay together in an unfaithful marriage, confusion over what married love is supposed to mean is usually at the root of a son's or daughter's emotional response. Such was the case with Tricia.

Tricia's Story: "Seeing both parents cheat, I told myself I would never get caught up in that cycle."

In addition to her confusion about what marriage means when marital commitments are broken, Tricia was also confused about which parent to align herself with, because the "guilty" party shifted from her father to her mother. Initially, her father was the unfaithful partner, and ten-year-old Tricia was forced into the inappropriate role of her mother's emotional caretaker. Now twenty-five, Tricia recalled what happened back then.

> *I was ten when I first remember hearing my mom say that my dad was with another woman. After that, whenever he was gone for a long time, she figured he must be cheating on her. I don't remember how long he would be gone; I just remember the aftermath and what it turned my mom into. She wasn't loving toward him anymore, and not trusting of him. My dad still tried to be loving with her. He tried to talk to her, but she wasn't receptive to him anymore.*
>
> *I was sympathetic toward her. I accrued some anger toward him, think-*

ing, You're not supposed to do that. I just remember that I didn't really talk to him. He'd come home from work and I'd just stay away from him. I'd just be with my mom all the time, asking her, "What do you need, Mom?" trying to please her. Or he'd do something, and I'd think, Oh, of course, you're hurting her feelings again.

Then the tables turned. When Tricia was fifteen, her father moved out of town for a few months to find work, and Tricia's mom took advantage of her newfound independence. Tricia explained that "since my mom had basically gone from her parents' home to being married at a young age, she never had a chance to sow her wild oats." Tricia seemed to want to justify her mother's behavior, and yet it caused her to experience intense anxiety, confusion, and anger as a teenager:

My mom would go out and leave me with her friends for the night. And then after a while, because it would turn into an every weekend thing, she just left me by myself. To this day she claims she wasn't doing anything bad. But I was aware and knew things that were going on. She would leave and I'd be thinking, How can you think that I don't know you're cheating on my father when you're not even telling me where you're going? You're not leaving a number for me to contact you. What if I need you? So I'm thinking, she's a mother—of course she should give me a number where she'll be . . . unless she's doing something inappropriate.

At that point, Tricia began to long for her father and to take his side in her parents' ongoing infidelity drama. She was hurt and outraged that her mother would not only leave her alone and lie to her about where she was, but also ask her to lie to her father:

When my mom was going out all the time, it pushed me toward my dad. We'd talk on the phone, and I wanted my dad at that time. I remember having to cover for my mom, because he would call and I would have to make up something about where she was. I couldn't believe she was asking me to do that, and I felt it was wrong that she was using me that way. I thought, You must be doing something wrong if you don't want my dad to know. And I just felt really bad for my dad. He was working in another state. He didn't want to be there . . . it's just that it was the only place he could find a job. So he was going through a lot, working to provide for us, and my mom was just partying it up, having fun.

Ten years later, Tricia still feels some confusion surrounding her mother's apparent secret life back then. She has no proof that her mother was unfaithful, but she doesn't understand why her mom can't be honest with her about what took place during that time.

To this day, I feel she did do something wrong. But for her to say, "I was with a man . . ." I don't think she'll ever tell me. I only brought this stuff up one time and she said, "Tricia, I have nothing to be ashamed about. I never disrespected your father." So I don't know what she meant—that she didn't do anything wrong? Or that she didn't feel bad about what she did? So I still don't know for a fact that she did do something. And my father doesn't know that either, because he was gone at the time.

Tricia's parents stayed together and, according to her, they are apparently happier now. Tricia believes both have been faithful for the past five years. As for her own relationships, Tricia told me that she is committed to a monogamous life, having witnessed the turmoil her parents went through. But, not surprisingly, in her relationship with her boyfriend, Tricia struggles with issues of trust. Because she took on the role of her mother's emotional caretaker when her father was unfaithful, and then later was forced to be her mother's co-conspirator, Tricia bears the burden of painful and confusing childhood experiences. She is now consciously trying to free herself from the mistrust she learned from her parents' behavior.

> *In my head, I'm thinking* men cheat—*that's just what happens. So it's a constant battle. I trust my partner, and I know that he's not the kind of person who would do that, but based on my environment and what I've seen, I tend to think,* that's just what happens. *My boyfriend knows that I've got this "baggage" in terms of my father's infidelity and my mother's suffering over it. So I let him know that maybe it's unfair for me to ask for this, but I need someone to work with me on these things. So if something makes me feel uncomfortable, we talk it out. If he's just hanging out with a friend and it really makes me feel uncomfortable, I'll let him know. Because the not knowing part? In my head, I could go crazy. He might just be gone for a few hours with a coworker, but in my head, I might be thinking,* They're in a hotel—*I could take it that far. That's from constantly hearing my mom being suspicious of my dad. So I'm trying to get away from that. This is my chance to have a healthy relationship.*

Even with a keen awareness of the emotional challenges she now faces, Tricia still finds herself mirroring the suspiciousness her mother once demonstrated so dramatically. And she recalls the evenings when, as a ten-year-old, she became the sounding board for her distraught mom:

> *I've been with my boyfriend almost a year. It's a monogamous relationship, we've told each other "I love you," and it feels like we're going to be together for a while. But now all these thoughts are occurring to me, like* Is he cheating on me? Is this inevitable? Will I push him into it? *With my mom, I'd look at her and I'd be thinking,* Don't act like that toward

my dad. Keep your man around. Accusing him of cheating on you isn't going to make him want to come toward you. *So I try to tell myself, Don't push him away by accusing him. It's torture.*

Tricia hasn't had the benefit of healthy role models when it comes to trusting, monogamous partners. And she still may be somewhat confused about the reasons for her father's unfaithfulness. Was he unfaithful because his wife was overly suspicious of him? Or were there other factors motivating him at the time? Which came first, her mother's doubts or her father's behavior? And since it seems likely that Tricia's mother also had extramarital affairs but hasn't been forthcoming about them with either Tricia or Tricia's father, Tricia has further reason to be confused and distrustful. She now worries that she may undermine her relationship due to her unfounded suspicions.

Still, Tricia is hopeful that she can overcome the trauma of having been the involuntary buffer between two unfaithful parents. Because she is aware of their mistakes and how much the whole family suffered for them, and because she is committed to avoiding the crises that nearly tore her parents apart, Tricia feels cautious yet optimistic:

> *Above all, I just don't want to fall into that. I've told myself, I'm going to respect myself. I'm not going to be my mother. I'm not going to marry a man like my father. I'm going to look at what they did to each other and not become part of that cycle.*

THE CONFUSION IN A PARENT'S LIES

Tricia's story reveals a core issue contributing to a child of infidelity's sense of confusion: a parent's lies. Aside from coping with the unsettling reality of ongoing parental infidelity, the lies and secrecy surrounding it can be profoundly disorienting for a child of any age. If parents lie, how can a child gain her bearings in the world? As Dr. Harriet Lerner explains in her book, *The Dance of Deception*, when children are not told the truth by their parents, they can't trust their own thoughts and feelings. She says, "We grow up assuming that our parents will not intentionally lie to us, or deliberately conceal information about things that matter. We take on faith the information they give us. . . . We expect straight answers, or, if not that, to be told that some things are private and will not be shared or discussed with us. If we are not told the truth, we cannot trust the universe—including our internal universe of thoughts, feelings, and perceptions."[11]

One of the reasons why unfaithful parents don't want to come right out and tell their child, "This may be difficult for you to understand, but I am having (or I had) an affair" is that they believe they are doing the right thing by hiding the truth. They may think that by revealing something "bad" about themselves, they will set a bad example for the child. While parents in an unfaithful marriage might believe in the old adage, what you don't know can't hurt you, being lied to can hurt children. While being told about a parent's "bad" behavior is certainly upsetting, if it is done in a sensitive, age-appropriate manner, it is less harmful to a child than living with the doubts and confusion created by a parent's lies.

Parents usually want to teach their children what is good for them, not necessarily what is true. But by hiding the truth, unfaithful parents create confusion by telling their children what they believe is "good" for them (e.g., Tricia's mom saying, "I never disrespected your father") while at the same time engaging in actions that contradict that "good" information—or, rather, disinformation. Being told one thing by your parent and knowing that the opposite is true results not only in confusion but anger and distrust. Just as Tricia sensed that her mother indeed had an affair ("To this day, I feel she did do something wrong"), children sense when they're being told a lie, even when parents attempt to cover it up. Attempting to deceive a child and pretending that everything is fine only compounds the confusion and emotional damage of parental infidelity.

Christina's Story: "My mom's attitude was, you get married for better or worse—if he cheats on you, that's just how men are."

Unlike Tricia, Christina was not deceived by her parents. She knew why they stayed together even though her father continuously had affairs: her mother expected her husband to be unfaithful and didn't believe his affairs were a reason for divorce. Nonetheless, Christina has struggled throughout her life with a sense of confusion over what marriage means when one parent is unfaithful and the other goes along with it.

As early as Christina can remember, her father came home however late he wanted to, and her mother wasn't allowed to ask where he had been or with whom. Her mother's acceptance of male infidelity is in keeping with the culture in which Christina's parents were raised, but Christina never believed in the cultural sanctioning of cheating husbands. In fact, her protest against married men having sexual affairs began when she was only five years old. She found boxes of condoms in her father's car and asked him what they were. He must have offered an explanation that defended his right as a man to be with other women.

Christina remembers her reaction:

> I was really disgusted. I was really hurt. I remember I told my father, "You shouldn't be looking at other women—you have my mom!" And my mom just laughed and said, "Don't worry, your dad can't do anything." She

just blew it off. My dad was very brazen. I remember when we'd be driving, he'd turn and look at women who were younger than my mother in such a leering, lustful way that it was very obvious. He didn't hide it. And I would hit him. I would always hit him in the arm and say, "Dad, don't do that—that's very rude."

It's interesting that while Christina's mother didn't seem to react to her husband's sexual betrayals, little Christina did. Regardless of the culture she had grown up in, something in her emotional makeup made her sense that a mother and father should reserve their affection for each other. Christina felt strongly enough about what she perceived as her father's "rudeness" to punch him in the arm and protest. Her response went deeper than simply telling her father that what he was doing was wrong. She told me that as a child she felt personally betrayed when her father had girlfriends or looked at women flirtatiously, "because I thought if he, as my father, was looking at women other than my mom, that must mean that I didn't mean that much to him either."

When she became old enough to start having an interest in boys, Christina says she consciously avoided contact with them, "because I knew I'd get hurt." Having learned from both of her parents that male/female relationships, including marriage, amounted to men betraying women, Christina swore off boyfriends throughout junior high and high school. Her mother had warned her that "men cheat— it's just the way they are," and Christina heeded the warning by steering clear of boys as a teenager. Then, in college, she dated a young man for about a year. When he eventually cheated on her, she was reminded of the hurt she had felt as a child over her father's infidelity.

Christina didn't marry that young man. Instead, she ended up marrying someone whom she had known in high school, someone who also cheated on her. When she went on to graduate school, her husband complained that she spent too much time studying and not enough time with him. Although she cooked and cleaned in addition to holding down a job and working toward her graduate degree, he used her alleged unavailability as a reason to cheat. Christina condemned her husband's infidelity, but she somehow bought into his argument that it was at least partially her fault.

I thought I must be doing something wrong [when he cheated on me the first time]. The entire time that I was married, I was afraid of being betrayed. When he and I would get into discussions about children or finances or whatever, I held my tongue because there was that fear of, "he cheated on me once before. If I push him too much he'll go off and do it again." Subconsciously, that was how I felt.

When her husband lost his job, he continued to be unfaithful while at the same time voicing concern that Christina was the one who might cheat. It seems his displeasure over her getting a graduate degree was based in part on his own insecurity. It was a blow to his ego to have his wife achieving lofty goals while he was floundering economically. And perhaps his affairs were an attempt to bolster his self-esteem. "He used to say to me, 'Oh, you're going to meet somebody better than me and you're going to cheat on me.' And that's when I started noticing his high level of insecurity."

If Christina had followed her mother's philosophy about accepting a man's natural need to stray, she would have stayed with her husband. But she not only felt she had more choices than her mother had, due to her professional status and ability to support herself, she ultimately refused to accept an unfaithful marriage. As often as she had questioned whether her own behavior might have instigated her husband's cheating, Christina was against the sanctioning of male infidelity on the grounds that it was simply "the way men are." She told me that she wished her mother had been more straightforward about what she wanted from her marriage. If she had, Christina says, "maybe my father would have changed a little bit, or at least his [womanizing] wouldn't have been as pervasive."

Christina's confusion growing up was about whether or not it was fair for men to be with other women and for their wives and families to accept it. As a little girl, she had never accepted it, but as a young woman she was involved with men who cheated on her, including the man she married. She is now divorced from him and is considering how she might change her expectations concerning male infidelity. She doesn't want to believe as her mother does that "all men cheat" and that to expect otherwise is to be naive. And yet she concedes that her past experience has colored her view of how men behave in relationships. She is now thirty-six and has met someone new, but she doesn't know if she's ready yet to fully trust a man.

When I left the marriage I wondered, Did I do something to make this person cheat on me? *And now that I have a new person in my life who wants to start dating me, I am putting that off, because I don't think I'm healthy enough to date someone and completely trust them. And I don't want to put any unresolved issues on this particular person. I can have as many friends as I want, but when it comes to the male species, there's something there. It's in my gut; it just doesn't let me let go of it.*

What is "in her gut" is the experience of having been a child of infidelity who felt repeatedly hurt and betrayed by her father's unfaithfulness. As much as she tried to protest what she saw going on in her own family, Christina learned from her parents that men cheat and women go along with it. That's the portrait of marriage that her parents drew for her. She would like to redraw that picture, and deepening her understanding of how she has been influenced by her parents' values is helping her in that struggle:

> *To this day, my mother tells me, "If you think you're going to find a man who will not cheat on you, who will not hurt you in that way, you're wrong. You'll never, ever find anybody, because that's the way it is. You just have to accept that they cheat, and that's it." I can see how [male infidelity] is perpetuated on both sides. One does it, and the other accepts that this is the way it's done in our culture. There is that whole thing in my parents' generation where it is acceptable for men to be this way. Not realizing that by perpetuating that idea, your daughter or son will either be a victim of it or will continue to perpetuate the same actions.*

Christina says she is firm in her desire not to maintain the marital philosophy her parents profess. When she left her husband, she made that very clear—in her own gracious manner:

> *When we broke up and I asked for the divorce, I told him, "You are who you are and I am who I am, so if this is the lifestyle you want to lead, I can't condemn it and I can't condone it. This is who you are and I wish you the best." I don't want to hold any anger toward him. I just can't be part of it. I can't continue living with someone who has such little respect for themselves and for me.*

WHEN INFIDELITY IS ONGOING IN YOUR MARRIAGE: ADVICE FOR PARENTS OF YOUNGER CHILDREN

Whatever your reasons for remaining in an unfaithful marriage, you need to communicate with your children in an age-appropriate way so that they can best understand the situation. If there is constant arguing, suspicion, and unhappiness surrounding the issue of infidelity, children will be upset and confused. And even if you think the issue is well hidden from them, it almost never is. Even very young children pick up on their parents' moods and emotions. If you deny that anything is wrong or fail to give a valid explanation for your anger, sadness, or withdrawal, you only add to a child's confusion.

Whether or not she explicitly knows about a parent's unfaithfulness, the overriding questions in a child's mind will likely be: "Why can't my parents love each other?" and "Why are they married if they don't love each other?" Not only will your child be anxious about the discord between you and your spouse and the affair(s) one of you is having, she will inherit a lasting image of what marriage means based on what she witnesses going on in your relationship. If that image is a confusing and unhappy one, wouldn't you want to do whatever you can to alter it?

My basic advice is to seek professional help to deal with the issues underlying your unfaithful marriage. When you and your spouse gain clarity about what is going on, you will be better able to deal with the situation and to communicate with your children about why the two of you are having problems.

WHEN INFIDELITY IS ONGOING IN YOUR PARENTS' MARRIAGE: ADVICE FOR ADULT CHILDREN OF INFIDELITY

If your parents are still married but one or both of them continues to be unfaithful, it is possible that you have come away with a confused notion as to what marriage means. Most people in this country expect that when they get married their relationship will be monogamous. And as surveys have shown, a majority of people believe that fidelity is part of the equation needed to develop trust as well as confidence that the relationship will last.

Although couples about to get married don't usually expect their mate to be unfaithful, infidelity is not uncommon. And when it occurs, it brings at least some degree of emotional chaos. Some couples deal with the chaos and work out their differences. As a child of infidelity, it is important for you to understand that the reasons for adultery vary, and a child—even an adult child—never knows the whole story behind why a parent is unfaithful. While it is not up to you to decipher the reasons for your parent's infidelity, it's important that you're clear as to what marriage means so that you have the opportunity to enjoy a fulfilling married life yourself, should you decide that is what you want.

When one or both spouses are having an intimate relationship with someone else, their marriage is no longer authentic. Because it lacks intimacy, it can't really be called a marriage. This doesn't mean that if one or both of your parents continues to be unfaithful that at some point in the future their situation can't change. But if one or both of them is having a sexual relationship with another person, at this time theirs is not a real marriage.

While it may be understandable for you to become cynical about love and commitment given your parents' history, remember that most people still believe in being faithful and committed to one person. And they usually do whatever they can to make their relationships work. When a couple marries, they promise to be loving and loyal; adultery is not part of the deal.

FIVE

I Have a Love–Hate Relationship with My Cheating Parent

I do not like what he did, but I still love him. It is not in his best interest for me to talk about it, and I do not want to lose my father, as bad as he is.

—Andrea, early twenties

My mom told me she didn't realize that her affair was the basis of my anger toward her. I told her, "I didn't know either, but now that it's all coming out, I realize it is."

—Julie, thirty-seven (recalling an affair her mother had when Julie was fifteen)

My dad told me [his sleeping with another woman] was none of my business; but the way I saw it, it was my business. I heard them having sex, and even at that age I thought, "What an ass!"

—Todd, thirty-three (reflecting on how he felt as a twelve-year-old)

I can't imagine my father walking me down the aisle one day to a man who is supposed to love me forever when he did not do that for my mother or my family. I love him and am angry at him at the same time.

—*Female survey respondent, twenty-four*

Most children of infidelity can't help but feel anger, sometimes even hatred, toward their unfaithful parent. They wonder how they can still respect or love someone who has not only broken the rules of marriage and lied about it but hurt the other parent and caused the whole family to suffer. A child of any age may believe it's impossible to feel the way they used to feel about their unfaithful father or mother. Although children are often told that their parents' marital problems are not their concern, and that nothing has changed between them and their cheating parent, children know better. Their feelings have changed, and very often those feelings are mixed—pulling the child in opposite directions.

In this chapter, we'll explore how children can feel intense anger toward their unfaithful parent and yet still need their love and support. As in Andrea's case, some children are afraid of losing contact with the parent who cheated and may even feel the need to protect that parent from feelings of shame, while at the same time hating his or her shameful behavior. Depending on their age, children of infidelity tend to reveal their ambivalent feelings toward the parent who cheated in a variety of ways. Young children can become anxious and insecure when they sense that their unfaithful parent is no longer the perfect hero he or she was once thought to be.

Needing and loving that parent while at the same time being unable to understand the parent's betrayal can be extremely stressful for young children. Their stress can manifest as problem behavior, regression, withdrawal, or other uncharacteristic conduct. School-age children take moral issues very seriously and are likely to angrily denounce the parent who cheats, but doing so can lead them to doubt whether the cheating parent will still love them, which in turn makes them feel insecure and uncomfortable. Teens and young adults identify with parents but are also beginning to form their own adult identity. Their cheating parent is a powerful role model about whom they now have intensely conflicted feelings. Since young people at this age are especially sensitive about parental hypocrisy, a father or mother's infidelity can push that button and incite even greater anger and resentment.

As difficult as it can be for a child of any age to hold conflicting emotions toward someone so important in their life, very often that is precisely the experience of a child of infidelity with regard to his or her unfaithful parent. Nora's story provides a poignant example of a child's need to hold on to the relationship with a cheating parent despite the anger and disappointment.

Nora's Story: "I have a lot of anger toward my dad, but I also have a soft spot for him."

Nora, now twenty-five, was fourteen when she found out that her father was cheating. He had been carrying on with a woman at work, whose husband called Nora's mother and told her about the affair. Nora's mom was outraged and confronted her husband immediately, but neither of them discussed it with their daughter. Instead, Nora found out by discovering a note from her mother to her father, bluntly stating, "You're an asshole for cheating." Nora says she became terribly anxious upon finding out that her dad was seeing another woman. More than anything else, she was terrified that this meant her parents might split up. She kept the discovery to herself until one day when her parents were fighting in front of her, and the argument became heated: "They were fighting, and my mom made some kind of veiled reference to the cheating. And I just said, 'You know, I know what's going on.' My mom wasn't very happy that I'd found out . . . I was upset at my dad, really upset."

Nora didn't directly express to her father how upset she was. It seems she was worried that if she confronted him, he might stop loving her. Or worse, he might leave—something she feared more than anything else. Nora says that once she discovered her father's infidelity, she paid more attention to her parents' fights and became more nervous every time one took place, because she was worried that it might mean they were breaking up. She determined that her role in the family would be that of a peacemaker:

> I would just try to calm their arguments down. I felt like I had to be the peacemaker because I didn't want my parents to separate. I think I'm like most kids who want to see their parents together, even if they might not be the right people for each other. So I was kind of a peacemaker, and I'd say, "Okay, if you're gonna fight, at least fight fair." I just didn't want to hear them argue. It was just too stressful.

Part of Nora's stress was due to her need to balance her unexpressed anger toward her father for having cheated with her love for him and her fear that he might leave. She coped with that stress by becoming a peacemaker. More than ten years later, Nora's parents are still together, and Nora still lives with them. Her boyfriend lives in her parents' house as well. Nora continues to take on the role of mediator when her parents get into fights, and she continues to worry that their arguments might escalate to the point where they could split up. As for her father's infidelity, Nora isn't certain if he has continued to be unfaithful. She does know that her mother recently discovered sexually suggestive e-mails between him and other women.

How does Nora feel today about her father being unfaithful to her mom? While she makes it a point to tell me that she loves her father very much and feels they have a better relationship than most fathers and daughters, she also concedes that she still holds a lot of anger toward him.

When I think about my dad cheating, I just cannot understand how you could cheat on the person you love, the person you married. And also, a lot of my anger toward my dad is about 'What kind of example are you giving your daughter? If I get married and my husband cheats on me, am I just supposed to be okay with that? Am I supposed to expect it—because my dad did it?' So I have a lot of anger toward my dad, but I also have a soft spot for him. I think we have a closer relationship than most fathers and daughters.

It seems that Nora tries hard to compartmentalize her anger toward her father so that it doesn't threaten either her love for him or her overall sense of well-being. She doesn't want her internal condemnation of her father to jeopardize their father-daughter relationship—or her parents' marriage—and yet, she hasn't fully resolved her feelings about his treatment of her mother:

There are moments when I get angry at him and I can't forgive him. But there are other times when he tries to make up for it. He'll say things that upset me, in terms of his views on women, and then he'll make up for it by saying things like, "I'm very proud of you because you're going to graduate school," so it's a really weird kind of love–hate relationship that I have with him.

While she and her father get into arguments about "his views on women," Nora still hasn't discussed with him how she feels about his having cheated on her mother. So perhaps the arguments she gets into with him also contain the anger she can't express directly. And yet she clearly doesn't want her anger toward him to dominate their relationship, which is why she is quick to add that he "makes up for it" with his acknowledgment of her academic accomplishments. It's as if she's telling herself, "I'm very angry at him for what he did, but he's really not so bad after all." Not wanting to lose him as a loving father and as the husband to her mother, she keeps her anger in check.

It is interesting that at twenty-five Nora not only lives with her parents but brought her own intimate relationship into their home as well. She says that part of the reason she and her boyfriend live with her parents is to save money, and that her boyfriend is okay with the setup; however, my sense is that Nora stays at home to protect her parents' marriage. In addition to her "love-hate relationship" with her father, the other overriding theme in our conversation was Nora's intense desire to have her family stay together. She probably doesn't want to move out of her family's home because she perceives her parents' relationship as still unresolved, and she seems to believe that if she doesn't live with them and no longer has some control over how her parents treat each other, the family could fall apart.

Adult children of infidelity like Nora sometimes have a problem leaving home because they feel responsible for their parents. Having taken on the role of peacemaker and mediator during the infidelity crisis, they continue to be there for their parents, often at the expense of their own relationships. Nora's love for her father and her anger toward him for putting the family at risk create a continuing emotional balancing act, which causes her a great deal of anxiety: "There was always anxiety whenever they would fight because I knew that my mom still had hostile feelings toward my dad. That was more just like my anxiety about what was going to happen. I wanted to make sure that my family stayed together. I think with time I'll let it go. I don't really know why he cheated. He said he was lonely at the time—my mother was going through law school when it happened. But there's part of me that thinks he's selfish. I think with time I'll learn to just let it go. It was an event that happened in life. It shaped me, it shaped our family in a certain way, but we've got to move on and learn from it."

While Nora states that she intends to let go of her angry feelings toward her father at some point, she is still holding that anger inside. And as numerous studies have shown, unreleased anger can adversely affect your health. For the sake of her physical and emotional well-being, it is time for Nora to talk to her father, not as an angry child but as an adult. She can express how she feels about his unfaithfulness as well as her hope that her parents stay together. Honestly expressing her feelings will clear the air and relieve Nora of a significant emotional burden.

Second, she can make the decision to live separately from her parents and relinquish her role as peacemaker, which will place the responsibility for her parents' marriage where it belongs—with her parents. As long as Nora continues to shore up their marriage by living with them and acting as a buffer, her parents are not fully confronting the problems in their relationship. And Nora is not free to live her own life. While she can hope for the best, she may need to be prepared to accept the reality that her parents' marriage may not last. If her parents stay together, it must be because they make that decision. Otherwise, her father may spend the rest of his days convinced that he's still married because of his daughter, and not because of his wife and a relationship that he values. If he and his wife fail to face their infidelity dilemma, his unfaithful behavior may in fact continue, which is just the opposite of what Nora intends by not expressing her angry feelings.

Paul's Story: "Will I be tempted to cheat like my father?"

Unlike Nora, Paul was a young adult before he learned the truth about his father: he had been a womanizer throughout his marriage to Paul's mom. Paul had always revered his dad, who he said was a good man, well liked and admired by others. But upon discovering that his father had always had affairs and was responsible for his mother's ongoing unhappiness in the marriage, Paul's opinion changed. He came away with not only conflicted feelings toward his father but also with mixed messages about how men ought to behave in a marriage. Paul told me he always wanted to be like his father—and yet it is still difficult for him to separate what he admires about his dad from what he rejects. In his late twenties, handsome, successful, and happily married for three years, one would not initially suspect that Paul is still deeply troubled by his past.

Neither of his parents offered him a clear explanation at the time, but when Paul was sixteen, they separated. Paul was very upset about the separation, which was instigated on the day of his father's birthday after one too many of his out-of-town trips. Paul remembers holding back from wishing his father a happy birthday that day: "How could I? It was a terrible day. But even though I was sixteen, I didn't know that my father had been unfaithful to my mother—or that his numerous affairs were the reason she insisted they split up. When I grew older, my mom told me that she knew my father wasn't always behaving well."

Interestingly, the phrase "behaving badly" was one that Paul used repeatedly to describe the infidelity of his father, uncles, and male friends, almost as if he were implying that men are like young boys whose occasional misbehavior or mischief is to be expected. Children, and especially teenagers, are anxious to learn the truth about their parents' code of ethics, the set of values by which they live. Paul

recounted the indirect way in which he discovered where his father
stood when it came to extramarital affairs.

*I remember my father was talking to me about a friend of his who was
always having problems with his wife because she constantly accused him
of having affairs. So my father was telling me that this man's wife was
really beautiful and the guy was really cool with his kids and everything,
and I asked my father, "But, what about the wife's accusations? How did
the guy actually behave?" and my father said, "He behaves pretty well."
And I said, "Wait a minute—what does that mean? He either behaves well
or he doesn't. You cannot behave pretty well." And my father told me,
"Pretty well means he goes to bed with some other woman from time to
time and he doesn't create a big mess of it." That made me understand something about my father. The way he saw his friend's relationship with other
women made me understand how he behaved himself.*

Paul told me that his father's infidelity made him feel conflicted
about how he should "behave" in his own marriage. On the one hand,
he was aware of how his mother had suffered due to his father's
affairs, but he was also aware that all of the men in his family carried
on as his father had, as did all his male friends. So it seemed to him
that male infidelity was normal. Still, at one point, not long after he
got married, Paul had so many doubts about whether or not he
should try to be a faithful partner that he consulted with his priest.

*After talking with my uncles and realizing that none of them were faith-
ful to their wives, and that none of the men I knew were either, I said to
myself, "Well, why should I [be faithful]?" I talked about this with the priest
who married me, and he told me, "Well, Paul, it's about levels of sin. For
example, if a top model like Claudia Schiffer knocked on your door and told*

you she wanted to be with you, well, I believe even God would understand."
That's what my priest told me.

So what I picked up on from the conversations I'd had with my uncles,
my friends, and the priest was that if you have to go and get laid with a
lady from time to time and that makes you act better at home—because you
aren't obsessed with that need—well then, do it. And if you feel guilty,
bring your wife flowers from time to time. But don't get too involved in
the affair, because then you can end up in a mess. If you're going to be upset
by the affair—and treat your wife badly and your kids badly—then that's
a worse problem than wanting outside sex and not allowing yourself to
have it.

Three years into his marriage, Paul is still conflicted about whether
or not to be faithful to his wife. While he hasn't yet given in to the
attraction he feels for other women, he admits that he has to set limits for himself with women he meets at work—otherwise, he's not
sure he would trust himself. When women colleagues and acquaintances approach him to go out for a meal, which he says happens
quite often, he makes lunch dates rather than dinner engagements.
That way there is less chance of drinking and of being seduced, which
is a real fear for Paul.

I would love to say that I will never be interested in another woman, but
I know I can't say that. And I'm really afraid of this. The way I see it, once
you start cheating, once you do it once, doing it the second and third time is
easier. I know it's something I want to stay away from—but I also know
that it's something that's very tempting.

Right now I can't say I won't end up behaving like my father. I cannot
say that. I fear ending up like him, and honestly, I think that fear has helped
me not to do this. Because whenever you relax and think you're not going

to fail on an exam, that's usually when you fail. But when you're really cautious, that's when you succeed. So this fear I have brings me hope that I won't give in to the temptations.

The pull to be with another woman is so great for Paul that he says he must constantly be on guard. For example, when he has to wait in a restaurant or other public place, he always brings something to read so that he won't be looking around, because he fears he won't be able to control the situation if a woman tries to seduce him. And at work he makes sure to hire only men or homely women so that he won't be attracted to them. He worries that if an attractive woman starts flirting with him, he won't be able to stop himself. Despite his precautions and his awareness that an affair would ruin his marriage—which he values and wants to preserve—Paul continues to worry that he will emulate his father's behavior.

Is Paul's fear of infidelity more intense because of his family history? Does he worry excessively about his wife's reaction to a possible affair because he remembers how unhappy his mother was? Would he be as tempted by other women if his father and uncles hadn't given in to that temptation so inevitably? My sense is that Paul is keenly aware of how destructive an affair can be and fears breaking up the family that he and his wife are now starting. He knows how bad it feels to be a child caught in a family torn apart by infidelity. While Paul often experiences the temptation to cheat, that temptation carries with it a red flag. Having paid the price of his father's infidelity, Paul wants to guard against his strong temptation to cheat so that his own family won't be forced to pay the same penalty.

Paul never stopped loving his father, but his admiration for him was considerably dimmed by the discovery that his father's affairs, however acceptable in the male culture to which he belonged, caused

Paul's mother to suffer—and caused Paul to doubt his own ideas about how a married man ought to behave. Paul was seventeen when his father passed away. As a teenager he had been angry at his father for cheating on his mother, but he couldn't continue to be angry at him after his death. He needed to make peace with his memory. So Paul accepted that his father was the way he was due to his family history and culture. Rationalizing his dad's behavior in this way, Paul is on good terms with his deceased father, but internally he continues to worry about whether or not he will follow his father's pattern with women. He has developed a way of coping with this fear by avoiding women whom he thinks might tempt him.

What Paul hasn't yet realized is that it is not the exposure to seductive women that results in cheating; rather, cheating is a decision one consciously makes. There is actually no need for Paul to avoid interesting or attractive women; what he does need to do, however, is to be clear in his own mind about his priorities and how he wants to protect the relationship with his wife. Paul cannot keep avoiding all potentially seductive women. At some point, his censor needs to come from within, and that is what will make him stronger.

THE URGE TO PROTECT A CHEATING PARENT

Some children of infidelity, especially those who are particularly sensitive, are able to empathize with a cheating parent even when that parent has inflicted pain on the betrayed spouse and the entire family. These children may sense that the parent feels ashamed, even though that parent has not asked for forgiveness or verbally expressed his or her feelings of shame. Being empathetic toward the parent who cheated doesn't mean that a child doesn't feel angry, sad, or ashamed of the parent's act of betrayal. Rather, the child seems to sideline those negative emotions to become understanding and conciliatory toward his or her unfaithful parent. In doing so, the child hopes, not only to help the parent in dealing with the pain he or she has caused, but also to prevent the parent from withdrawing his or her parental love or leaving the family altogether.

Andrea, in her early twenties, personifies the child who takes on the role of protector of an unfaithful parent. She talks about intuiting what her father must be feeling and reveals what she has decided to do to protect him from his own guilt and shame, which, according to her, he cannot face. Part of Andrea's agenda is to make sure her father doesn't withdraw from her and leave her without the fatherly love she still sorely needs.

I know that my father is ashamed of what he did to my mom, but he would not admit it. He avoids facing it, and if I bring it up, he will stop seeing me, as he is not able to face it. I know he regrets what he has done, as he was totally selfish and inconsiderate. And I know, too, that he did not know how to repair the situation. He is ashamed for having dealt with guilt so poorly!

I feel that I need to protect my father, because he is getting old and he regrets what he did. He hurt my mother and hurt us (my sister and me). He is trying to do everything possible not to realize how much pain he inflicted on us, but he does not do the right things. I would expect that he would stay around us, that he would do everything to be a good father, but as he is ashamed, he avoids seeing us, he avoids the family that he destroyed, he avoids facing the pain he incurred.

My sister is strong enough to tell him what she has on her mind. I cannot do that. He is so ashamed that I need to make him feel I am on his side, so he could have someone to rely on. He is actually lonely, and he is my

*father. I do not like what he did, but I still love him. Still, I do not want
to open up, because he would pull away due to shame. It is not in his best
interest for me to talk about it, and I do not want to lose my father, as bad
as he is.*

It is interesting—and sadly touching—that Andrea feels the need
to rescue her father. It is clear that she feels a responsibility to help
him handle his pain, to parent him in a sense. Behind her actions is
a belief that her father doesn't know how to handle his own sense of
guilt and that she must therefore take charge of the situation. At the
same time, it is evident that Andrea still feels considerable anger
toward her father, which she keeps to herself for fear that he cannot
deal with it. So she is depriving herself of the benefit of openly
expressing her feelings about her father's betrayal to make sure that
he doesn't fall apart emotionally. She says that "it is not in his best
interest for me to talk about it," and yet she clearly believes that it
would not be in her best interest to express her feelings to him. If she
were to do that, she says, she might lose him. And "as bad as he is,"
Andrea doesn't want to take that risk.

As was the case with Nora, Andrea is afraid of losing the relationship with her father. But I don't believe that will necessarily happen
if she talks to him openly and expresses both her anger over what he
has done as well as her wish to continue the father-daughter relationship. Not only did Andrea's father destroy Andrea's dream of having the traditional family, but according to her, he also destroyed a
marriage that he valued. Andrea's father is the kind of man who
doesn't want to talk about what hurts, especially if he is the one causing the pain. But is it really in his best interest not to talk about it?
Avoiding the reality of what he has done may be hurting him even
more than bringing these issues out into the open, especially since

Andrea loves him so much and wants their relationship to continue. Sometimes children of infidelity feel that they need to withhold their angry emotions because they sense that their parents can't handle them. But in my opinion not talking about the infidelity and failing to express how they feel is definitely not in the best interest of either Andrea or her father. Just like Nora, Andrea needs to talk to her father and disclose what is in her heart to preserve the relationship with him.

ONE DAUGHTER IS ANGRY, THE OTHER IS CONCILIATORY

Often in a family coping with an infidelity crisis, one child will respond to the betraying parent in one way, while another child has a very different reaction. Fifteen-year-old Abby and her thirteen-year-old sister, Kayla, are a case in point. Abby is vehemently angry at her father for having cheated on her mother. She told me that she feels disgusted by his actions and ashamed of the person he has revealed himself to be. She wants nothing to do with him at all and has turned down his offers to sit down and talk to her and explain himself. Abby's mother has told her, "the situation is just between your dad and me," but Abby responds angrily, saying, "That's not true! I am involved, too!"

Meanwhile, Abby's younger sister, Kayla, acts completely different toward her father. Ever since his affair was brought to light, Kayla has tried to be especially nice to her dad, hoping to smooth things over and prevent a breakup between her parents. Her fear of her parents splitting up is greater than whatever unexpressed feelings of distaste, disappointment, or anger she might have. If there is a cold silence at the dinner table, Kayla will try to engage her father in an upbeat conversation. She makes it a point to enlist his help with her homework and jokes around with him when they're working on it together. All of this cozy togetherness infuriates Abby, who believes that Kayla has sided with the enemy.

While their parents are in the process of deciding what to do about the infidelity crisis, Kayla is essentially seducing her father into staying with the family, and Abby continues to express her outrage. Both sisters' responses are related to a shared belief that their mother is incapable of handling the situation. Since they both assume that their mom was unable to prevent their father from having an affair, they likely believe that she will not be able to deal with the consequences. In the meantime, one sister communicates her fury while the other tries to lovingly convince their father to stay.

As sometimes happens with siblings in families where infidelity has occurred, Kayla and Abby are likely expressing their ambivalence toward their cheating parent by acting out opposing emotions. I expect that sometime in the future, the sisters' responses may switch; Kayla will convey her anger, while Abby will be on better terms with her dad. While the parents are still deciding what to do with their marriage, the girls' attitudes toward their father will likely remain fixed; however, if their father decides to leave, Kayla could become very mad at him and feel personally rejected. And as Abby sees her sister becoming angry, she may become more understanding of her father, because she'll no longer have as strong a need to be irate to counterbalance Kayla's sweetness. At this point, as they are waiting to see what will transpire in their parents' marriage, each girl's emotional response toward their dad is calibrated according to the other's reaction.

Whatever their parents decide to do, it is important that Kayla and Abby's father apologize to each of them for having betrayed their mother and them. Children of infidelity need an apology, as they have been betrayed, too, but not all unfaithful parents are able to apologize. Some lack remorse, others cannot handle the shame, and others simply don't know how to approach their children about such a sensitive subject. But an apology can help to defuse the anger and the hurt that children like Kayla and Abby cannot help but feel.

Julie's Story: "For twenty years, I didn't realize how angry I was at my mom."

Sometimes a child of infidelity is unable to feel the anger toward a betraying parent, let alone express it. When monitoring and sympathizing with a parent's feelings take precedence over one's own responses and emotions, a child's anger can become buried for years. That is what happened in Julie's case.

Now thirty-seven years old, Julie told me that her mother had always treated her more like a girlfriend than a daughter. They were only twenty years apart, and when Julie was in her early teens, her mother began confiding in her about how unhappy she was in her marriage. A few years later, she told Julie about a young man at work with whom she could communicate far better than Julie's father. Julie described her father as "a very private man who never really had any friends," whereas her mother was outgoing, fun-loving—and frustrated that her marriage provided so little opportunity for fun or companionship. At the time, Julie sympathized with her mom's frustration and easily understood why she would develop a friendship with a coworker who she could comfortably talk to. But the scenario became more complicated as Julie's mother became instrumental in turning this young man into Julie's first teenage crush.

My mom started telling me how nice it would be if this young man and I could go out together. She'd say, "He's so nice, he's good-looking, he's going to college—I think he'd be great for you to go out with." So he was my very first date, ever. I was fifteen. She set it up so that this young man, who was five years older than me, and I went out on my first date. He was about twenty, and my mom was thirty-five at the time. I was in love with him. I thought I was, anyway—after one date!

I realized over the next few months that I was infatuated with him, not only from being with him on that date, but because of the stories that I'd heard from my mother about him. I really thought maybe I could have a future with this boy, that maybe I could continue dating him or something. But it was not long before I realized that this wasn't about me and the boy anymore. It was about my mom and him. She was having an affair with him.

Julie went out only once with the young man who her mother ended up having an affair with, but the betrayal she suffered was profound and confusing. Yet she didn't talk about it with her mother for two decades. In fact, her feelings about what her mother had done were unclear even to Julie. Since Julie had taken on the role of her mother's best friend and confidante, her allegiance to her mom took precedence over acknowledging or expressing her own angry, hurt feelings:

At the time I was thinking we were more like friends than a mother and a daughter. And we had become such confidantes at that time that I almost turned against my father. I thought of him as the bad guy. I saw him as not providing her with the love and attention she needed. When she started having this affair with the man that I loved, then definitely I felt awful—I felt she had betrayed me and my dad. But I couldn't express my feelings toward her. She was going through such a hard time—I wanted her to be happy. So I couldn't express that I was hurt and felt betrayed. I couldn't express how angry I guess I probably was at that time, without realizing it.

After that, I started having sexual intercourse, when I was fifteen, with young men at school who I barely knew. Looking back, it was probably just my way of acting out what was happening at home.

Julie described how, as a teenager, she had numerous sexual relationships with boys for whom she had no feelings. All the while, she repressed the anger toward her mother for having betrayed both her and her father. And she continued to be there for her mom, listening to complaints about her marriage to Julie's dad: "We never talked about the whole situation with this young man. Our discussions were always centered around the fact that she couldn't make it work with my dad. There were just so many troubles, so many problems with communication in the marriage. And that my dad never wanted to have fun with her, he never wanted to take her out, never wanted to take her dancing—that kind of thing. So we never really touched on the fact that she had had this extramarital affair. It was just that period where she kind of temporarily lost it."

On the one hand, Julie seemed to excuse her mother's affair, accepting the rationale that her mom's unhappiness led her to temporarily "lose it." On the other hand, Julie acted out her hurt and anger by punishing herself with degrading sexual encounters throughout her mid- to late teens. Neither she nor her mother referred to the affair that caused such an upheaval in both of their lives (as well as that of Julie's father). After the affair, Julie's parents divorced. Julie's mom eventually remarried, and Julie spent years acting out her confusion and anger in unhealthy relationships with men. Either she gave herself sexually to men she didn't care about, or she got involved with men whom she cared for but who cheated on her. At twenty-three, after hitting bottom and realizing that she wanted a healthy relationship, Julie met someone who is loving and trustworthy; the two have been married for eleven years. Julie says that her husband helped her to "go through this journey of repairing myself and acknowledging that I'm worth more than what I had been doing to myself with all of those men."

But what about the repressed anger toward her mother? Julie told me that twenty years after her mom's affair with the young man who was Julie's first date, her anger finally surfaced unexpectedly during a phone conversation:

> *My mom was confiding in me again about problems she was having with her second marriage, and I was just not in the mood that day. We were on the phone, and I was very abrupt with her, telling her, 'Just do something! Leave your husband or get over it.' She was hurt. She said, "Why are you so mean to me sometimes?" And I finally had the courage. I cried, and I told her, "You know I've thought a lot about this, and I don't know why I'm so angry at you at times, why I get so annoyed with you. But I think it all stems from the fact that back when I was fifteen, I lost my trust and my faith in you." And she said, "What are you talking about?" And I said, "I've never told you this, but I was really, really hurt that you had the affair with the boy that I, in my head, was in love with. I only went out with him once, but to me it was a whole fantasy, that I had a relationship with this boy. And you started dating him. So it was a betrayal against me and my father. And I guess the fact that you are not a trustworthy person really makes me mad."*

Along with the release of her long-hidden anger, that milestone phone call also revealed the empathy that Julie still feels for her mother. Although Julie is finally able to own her angry feelings about her mom's betrayal, she still demonstrates a compassionate concern for her mother's "issues." All those years of being her mother's confidante have left their mark:

> *My mom told me she didn't realize that the affair was the basis of my anger toward her. I told her, "I didn't know either, but now that it's all coming out, I realize it is." And sure enough, in the last year, I just feel like this burden has been lifted off my shoulders. When I talk to her, I can see her as an individual, a human being who has issues, and that she's working hard to become a better person. I'm not the anger-filled daughter that she had before. Now I feel I can approach her with more compassion, but it's taken so long to get here. I still struggle with it. Every now and then I'll get short with her, and I'll realize, "Okay, I know what this is about." So I think our relationship is better because of the work I've done in trying to figure out why our relationship has been so strained.*

It's interesting that, as a teenager, Julie was forced to see things solely from her mother's perspective, thereby denying her own angry response to her mom's affair. Because she was so closely enmeshed in her mother's life, Julie was unable to find her own direction. While teenage girls her age generally date boys to discover more about themselves, Julie engaged in sex with various partners largely as a confused and angry reaction to her mother's affair. After many years of acting out that anger, initially in self-destructive relationships with men, and later in being "short" with her mom for seemingly no good reason, Julie was finally able to be straight with her mother. The underlying anger was about the betrayal she had endured as a fifteen-year-old, which her mother never acknowledged or apologized for:

On the phone that day, it just all started pouring out of me. I realized that twenty years of my life have been spent being angry at her, and not even knowing what the root of it was. The anger and frustration every time we spoke—it was really about that unfaithfulness, that disrespect. There are other ways she could have handled her unhappiness with my father.

She put me in a situation where I had to be the grown-up and help her. And that's also been a source of great frustration in my life. She's my mother. She should be my role model. She should be my mentor. I had all these expectations of what a mother should be, and yet she can't be that. She's always been the unfaithful one. She's the one that I can't trust anymore.

Julie's challenge now is to mourn the loss of the mother she always wished she had had. Her mom seriously erred as a parent when she shared intimate information about her marital relationship with her young daughter, when she betrayed both her daughter and her husband by having an affair with the young man Julie dated, and when she encouraged a "girlfriend" connection with Julie rather than a mother-daughter relationship. Julie's mom will probably never be the mentor Julie would have wanted, but parents are rarely what we expect them to be. Finally pinpointing where her anger originated and openly expressing that anger to her mom has helped Julie to clear the way toward a more honest relationship with her mother—and with herself.

HOW DOES UNRESOLVED ANGER AFFECT THE RELATIONSHIPS OF ADULT CHILDREN OF INFIDELITY?

Anger that originates with parental infidelity doesn't dissipate on its own. Parents need to help their younger children deal with it, and young adults need to take responsibility for their own healing so that their anger doesn't persist and fester. Often a professional counselor or psychologist can help in this regard. When an adult child has been unable to work through the anger toward an unfaithful parent, it usually spills over into his or her intimate relationships.

Todd and Sharon are both in their early thirties. Their stories are similar in that each has lived with anger toward their respective fathers, who were both serial cheaters. Todd says he has lost all respect for his father and expresses few positive feelings toward him. Sharon talks about how much pain her father's womanizing has caused her and her mother. At one point she even told me that although she still loves her father, she wishes he would die so that his behavior will no longer cause her mother so much grief. Neither Sharon nor Todd is free of their anger toward their betraying parents, and that charged emotion continues to affect each of their marriages. Their stories offer insight into how unresolved anger toward a parent who cheats can linger for decades.

Sharon's Story

Sharon's father has been having affairs throughout his marriage to Sharon's mother. Sharon was six years old when she first found out that her father had children from another woman. She discovered this life-changing reality the day her dad first took her to play with her half sisters while he had sex with their mom:

> I remember being shocked—and mad. Because I was a little girl, I didn't know everything that was going on, but I knew that whatever it was, it was wrong. My father told me, "Go outside and play—these are your sisters," and I said, "What, Daddy?" and he said, "These are your sisters," and we were expected to be instant friends. While he was upstairs having sex with

their mom, I was downstairs with my half sisters, who I never even knew existed before that day. That first day I was really scared, and then each time we would stay a little bit longer. And then one time he made me stay the night there. And I don't know how my mom said yes or why she said yes, but she agreed to it, and I just remember being at their house and hating every minute of it.

Sharon's mother wasn't happy about her husband's continual affairs, but she put up with his womanizing in part because she is devoutly religious, and her religion prohibits divorce. As Sharon got older, she became more aware of her father's ongoing sexual relationships, and her anger intensified. "By the time I became of dating age," she told me, "I was so cynical. I was so jaded." Sharon got married before she turned eighteen, even though she says that she didn't really want to; rather, she claims that her husband talked her into it. Although her husband has never cheated on her, Sharon's assumption continues to be that "all men cheat." It is apparent from her comments that Sharon's anger toward her father has led to some very pessimistic attitudes about marriage, as well as about men in general and her husband specifically:

Before we got married, I would tell my husband, "Why do you want to get married? It's just a piece of paper; it has no value. It would be easier if we just live together, because when you get tired of me, you can just pack up and get out." And now I tell him, "If you want to go screw around, you're more than welcome to pack your stuff and get out, because I'm not going to be married to a man who screws around." And my husband will say, "No, I'm different. I won't do that," and I tell him, "You're all the same. All men are the same."

Sharon's anger toward her father is so great that she generalizes that rage toward all men, including her husband, who has been faithful to her for thirteen years. Yet Sharon continues to taunt him with her belief that he will cheat on her one day. "It's just a matter of time," she tells him. The sting of her father having had illegitimate children with several other women (not only the ones Sharon remembers meeting when she was six) remains with Sharon as well, which is why she demanded that her husband prevent such a nightmare from happening in her own family.

After our daughter was born, I made my husband get a vasectomy. I told him, "If you screw around, do it without spreading your seed around like my father did." Now I joke with my husband and say, "Ha, ha—today your girlfriend called me to tell me she's pregnant with your baby. I'm gonna laugh in your face while I'm putting your clothes in the barbecue, cause I'm gonna burn them." And he'll tell me, "Why do you say things like that? You're so mean to me," and I'll say, "No I'm not, I'm just speaking the truth, because we know it's gonna happen; it's just a matter of if I bust you or not. If you get caught or not." I hate the fact that I am this cynical, but I can't help it.

I asked Sharon what it would feel like if she allowed herself to be less cynical, and she conceded that she might then feel more vulnerable, a state that frightens her. The anger she still feels toward her father not only makes Sharon less open to receiving her husband's love, it also prevents her from feeling the sadness about what happened to her as a child—a sadness that she is only sometimes willing to express.

I'm just so angry at my father. And I'm sad because I was a child, and he made me see things and he made me do things that children shouldn't have to do. I shouldn't have had to lie to my mom because he was out screwing around. I shouldn't have had to be forced to play with his illegitimate children and be forced to be nice to these whores and then have to turn around and not tell my mom. That was really, really wrong. But I don't think he ever understood it. And I don't think he still does. And I don't think he cares that he hurt us.

I think about the day when my dad will pass, and I hate to say it, but I look forward to it, because it will give my mother freedom. And as much as I love him, I hate him. I hate him very much.

Later in our conversation, Sharon mentioned that she still loves her father, despite all the anguish he has caused. Her hatred and anger began to give way to sadness:

He's sixty-seven years old, but my mom found a prescription for Viagra in his office one day, and at this point I told my husband, 'I can't get angry anymore.' [She starts crying] I don't get as angry as I used to. I just feel sad. I feel sad for my mom . . . I love my dad, but I hate what he did so much.

Although Sharon claimed that she doesn't get as angry as she used to, I had heard her anger flare up throughout our interview. I think she still holds a lot of rage toward her father, and much of it gets shifted over to her husband. Sharon told me that she has had conversations with her father in which she has vented her feelings. But these conversations only make her angrier because her father tells her that she needs to accept that all married men are unfaithful, that he is just a normal man, and that it is only a matter of time before her husband will cheat on her.

How might Sharon begin to constructively deal with some of the anger that such conversations bring up? Is it possible for her to rid herself of the fury she feels toward her father, and in so doing eradicate the bitterness and cynicism she demonstrates toward her husband? I told Sharon that when her father insists all men are unfaithful, he is actually justifying his behavior—not stating a fact. In fact, the majority of married men in this country do not cheat on their wives. I told her, "Whenever your dad's words play out in your mind, remind yourself that 'these are my father's ideas, not the absolute truth.'" I suggested that it might be a good idea for her to have a journal in which she can write down the angry thoughts she still has about her father, so that those feelings don't spill over into her communication with her husband. Sharon's husband knows that she has been traumatized by her father's continual infidelity, and Sharon admits that her husband has been a caring mate. So her marital challenge is twofold: to honestly communicate with her husband about the struggle she's going through, rather than lashing out at him; and to acknowledge that all men are not like her father.

I told Sharon that if she is tempted to make insinuations about her husband's probable infidelity, she can remind herself that "this is only a feeling I have, not an absolute truth." If she finds that she cannot stop herself from wrongfully accusing her husband of wanting to cheat on her, I suggested that Sharon immediately tell him something like this: "I'm sorry I just said that, because I really don't mean it. As you know, I'm still trying to resolve my old issues about my dad's infidelity. These angry feelings are about my dad; I know you are different."

As for how she might defuse the anger toward her father, I suggested that Sharon think about her father as a person with an addiction—like an alcoholic. He hasn't merely fallen in love with another woman or had one or two affairs; he has had numerous affairs and illegitimate children with several women. If Sharon can understand that her father's behavior is like an addiction, she will not only feel less angry about it, she will realize that not all men are addicts. And she can tell herself, "I am not married to an addict."

When she is able to better understand her father's behavior and put his ongoing infidelity into a sharper, more realistic, perspective, chances are that Sharon's anger will diminish. In the meantime, she can work on repairing her relationship with her husband by declining to take out her anger on him.

Todd's Story

Todd's father had cheated on his mother, and his parents divorced when Todd was young. His father remarried and continued to have extramarital affairs, one of which Todd was asked to lie about. Todd had a close relationship with his stepmother—he told me he had a better relationship with her than with his father—and he was furious that his father asked him to betray her. More than twenty years after the incident, Todd's anger was very much out in front as he described what happened.

I was a twelve-year-old kid away for the weekend with my dad and my uncle, and a female shows up. So she ends up staying the night there—and he sleeps with her! He knows that I know about sex, that I know what he did was wrong—and he still did it! And then he expects me not to say anything! He got very p.o.'d that I was going to tell my stepmom—almost like I was betraying him. But I saw that he didn't respect me—he didn't hold me in high regard. My dad told me it was none of my business, but the way I saw it, it was my business. I heard them having sex, and even at that age I thought, What an ass!

At the age of twelve, Todd was able to come right out and tell his father that he didn't approve of what he'd done. He also threatened to tell his stepmother the truth if his father didn't level with her, which his father did. Still, Todd told me, "I lost a lot of respect for my father because of that incident." His dad continued to have affairs, and Todd's anger about it continued as well. As for his own relationships, at eighteen Todd became the victim of infidelity when his first serious girlfriend cheated on him. His reaction to her betrayal was overwhelming.

I was deeply hurt from my first relationship when she cheated on me. She was my first love. It was very sexual, and in reality I didn't know what love was. I thought I was in love, but when she deceived me, and I actually caught her, it was the most devastating feeling—uncontrollably—I mean I was just . . . every emotion went through my head. I was capable of doing anything. I was capable of killing someone—I could feel it. And I did not like not having control over my feelings. And I thought to myself, This is why people kill spouses—because they can't control themselves.

That affected me so drastically that I never wanted it to happen again. In fact, I didn't get into any serious relationship for two years after that because I was scared to death that they would hurt me again. I've been with women who I thought I loved and wanted to be with, and was loyal to them, and then they cheated on me. And it was devastating. It was one of the things that I wanted to avoid at all costs.

Although at the time Todd didn't associate his unfaithful girlfriends with his experience as a child of infidelity, I explained to him that he may have been unconsciously attracted to young women with whom he could reenact the infidelity drama he had been involved in as a pre-teen. Perhaps Todd's sense of being unable to control his feelings upon discovering his first girlfriend's betrayal was closely connected to the intense anger he felt as a twelve-year-old unable to control his father's betrayal. After several breakups resulting from girlfriends cheating on him, in his twenties Todd went through a period of sleeping around a lot, which only made him feel guilty and lonely.

I did a lot of partying and running around and chasing women and all that, but it was just a lonely feeling—sleeping with women and coming home and waking up with someone you don't even know who they are. It's an extremely lonely feeling. I started feeling guilty and very lonely, and I said, "I can't do this anymore, this has to stop. I need to change my life." I wanted to meet someone and be loyal to her. I wanted to have a family.

Todd got married, had children, and now points to his marriage as the most important thing in his life. After growing up in two unstable homes—with his single mom who had boyfriends in and out of their home and with his dad who was repeatedly unfaithful to his stepmother—Todd craved a family life that provided love and stability. He feels strongly about guarding against the kind of emotional chaos that he lived through as a child of infidelity, and that he experienced as a betrayed partner. While Todd and his wife have created a satisfying life together, it is apparent that he still harbors unresolved anger toward his father. The upsetting ordeal of having to witness his father's sexual affair still resonates powerfully with Todd. His angry feelings came out once again when he described why he could never cheat on his wife, even though most of his friends cheat on theirs. The incident from years ago again came alive for Todd, as if it had happened only yesterday:

I've been tempted to cheat since I've been married. But what always stops me is, I think if I do something like this, just this one time, I would lose my wife, I would lose my children, and then, again, I'm back into being

*unstable, single, and I would be hurting somebody that I dearly love. That
is unacceptable. I could never see my wife go through something like that.
I could never see her hurt like that because I've seen what it does. I watched
my stepmother, who I have a lot of respect for—she was very good to me—
and I watched her cry because of what my dad did. And it infuriated me.
That's why I told him, "If you don't tell her, I'm going to." After that, my
dad and I didn't have a very good relationship because [in his eyes] I'd broken that sacred son and father thing. But the way I saw it was, this guy
who cheated on my mom and broke up their marriage, and then he was
gonna get away with cheating on my stepmom? I don't think so! I couldn't
look at my dad after that—he made me sick for a long time.*

Todd has struggled to create a married life that is the extreme
opposite of his father's. He appreciates what it means to have a stable, intimate relationship with his wife and is painfully aware of the
damaging effects infidelity can have on a family. But adamantly
shunning his father's adulterous lifestyle has not lessened Todd's
anger toward him. How might he diminish that anger now, as an
adult? I believe what Todd needs to do is accept that he and his father
will never share the same values concerning women and marriage,
while at the same time reestablishing a connection to his father based
on other aspects of their lives. They could still share something as
simple as a weekend meal, or as profound as a concern for Todd's
children. I think once Todd realizes that his father is who he is
because of his own upbringing and personality, he may finally be
able to forgive him. And with forgiveness comes the dissolving of
one's anger.

We will deal in depth with forgiveness in the last chapter, but essentially it involves understanding why a person behaves as he does while
also letting go of your anger toward that person so that you are no

longer burdened by it. Forgiving his father doesn't mean that Todd excuses him for what he did; rather, it means that Todd will be free to enjoy his own life as a less angry person.

DEALING WITH YOUR YOUNG CHILD'S ANGER TOWARD THE CHEATING PARENT

I encourage you to give your children the opportunity to vent their anger toward the cheating parent if, in fact, that is what they are feeling. Of course, be open to hearing whatever other feelings they might have about the infidelity scenario. Young children do not understand whatever reasons parents may have for engaging in extramarital relationships. They are still learning about the world, and for them there is only right and wrong and nothing in between. A young child of infidelity likely will feel angry, betrayed, and antagonistic toward the cheating parent, while they may resent and be angry toward the betrayed parent as well. The best thing that both parents can do is to remain emotionally and physically present to the child or children, to ameliorate their sense of betrayal. With that general advice in mind, here are guidelines for how to deal with your child's anger and ambivalence toward the parent who cheated.

- Be willing to listen to what your child has to say, even if it is expressed with anger and hurt. Understand that anger is a normal human reaction, and when it is expressed appropriately, it can be spiritually healthy.
- Listen to your child's angry feelings with respect, even if this means putting aside your own emotional distress.
- If you are the betrayed parent and your child expresses under-

standing or love or longing for the cheating parent, allow them to do so without interjecting your own bias.

- Listen to your child's questions and respond with the truth, even when it may not be pleasant. Lying to your child perpetuates the lies of infidelity, which is the worst thing you can do to him or her. This is the time to be up front and direct, an approach that does not imply giving details.
- There is no need to insist that a child talk about what has happened, but being a good listener lays the foundation for your child's questions and venting of feelings.

DEALING WITH ANGER TOWARD YOUR CHEATING PARENT: ADVICE FOR ADULT CHILDREN OF INFIDELITY

It is important to speak out instead of holding on to your anger. The process of speaking from the heart and articulating your thoughts helps you to clarify issues and reflect on your deepest feelings. Whether you do so in a conversation with your cheating parent or in a therapeutic setting with a counselor or psychologist, expressing your anger and pinpointing where those feelings originate is an initial step toward healing. Often an expression of anger or hatred leads to deeper feelings of sadness, hurt, and fear. But venting the anger is a necessary part of the process of dealing with all of your emotions concerning your parent's infidelity. Working to understand the emotional impact of your parent's betrayal presents a significant opportunity for healing.

As we'll discuss in the last chapter, learning to forgive the parent who cheated is the final step in releasing your anger.

SIX

Is It My Job to Comfort and Side with My Betrayed Parent?

When my mother left my father for a man she had been having an affair with, I felt so sorry for my dad. He was lost. After Mom left him, we spent a lot of time together. We'd go out to eat every Saturday night, and I would be thinking of ways to cheer him up, to get his mind off Mom. Then I realized—or my therapist helped me realize—that spending almost all of my free time with him wasn't really doing him or me any good. I was twenty-one and I'd never had a serious boyfriend. I had to start thinking of myself.

—*Suzanne, twenty-six*

A betrayed parent is often left feeling dejected, depressed, and unloved. In the demoralizing aftermath of a spouse's infidelity and rejection, the love of a child, whether they're five or twenty-five, can be a tremendous comfort. But sometimes betrayed parents cross the line between spending time with their children and depending on those children to meet their own emotional needs. When children of infidelity are called upon to become their betrayed parent's emotional caretaker or surrogate mate, an inappropriate burden is placed on that child.

Sometimes the unfaithful spouse is the one to encourage the child to fill a role for which he or she is unsuited. One father told his preteen daughter, "I know that what I did hurt your mom very much. She is suffering now and needs you to be there for her." But if a child is expected to attend to and console a distraught parent whose spouse has cheated, who will be available to attend to that child's emotional needs? One of the issues many children of infidelity brought up in their survey responses was that betrayed parents were often unavailable as parents. Too consumed by their own anger or unhappiness, they were unable to provide the nurturing and support their children needed.

The issue of conflicting loyalties may also come into play when a child of infidelity is obliged to be the caretaker of an emotionally wounded parent. Some betrayed parents expect their children to share their disdain for the unfaithful spouse. When their kids speak lovingly of the cheating parent or want to spend time with him or her, they are accused of being disloyal. With such expectations placed upon them, it's no wonder that children may come to resent the betrayed parent.

Another matter that survey respondents referred to was the betrayed parent's indirect responsibility for the infidelity. Some adult children said that their betrayed father or mother was to blame for being unable to prevent the other parent from cheating, for essentially pushing the cheating parent into an affair. One respondent noted that her betrayed father "never really showed my mom that he loved her—was never affectionate, never demonstrative—so she had to go looking for love from someone else."

In this chapter we'll hear from children of infidelity who felt stuck in the role of caretaker to a betrayed parent, who were offended by the betrayed parent's bitterness toward the cheating parent, or who held their betrayed parent accountable for the other parent's unfaithfulness. Throughout the chapter, I will offer my insight and advice as to how such resentments can be prevented by parents in the midst of an infidelity crisis or dealt with by adult children still grappling with these difficult issues.

Suzanne's Story: "I became my dad's stand-in partner."

Suzanne had always assumed her parents were happy. They had met in high school and were each other's first love. According to Suzanne, they rarely fought and were affectionate with each other in public. But behind the pleasant facade, Suzanne's mother had grown dissatisfied with her marriage. In her midforties she began an affair with a man she met in an evening art class. Suzanne was away at college when she received the news that her mother was leaving her dad to live with this man.

When my dad called and told me what was going on, his voice was barely audible. I was so shaken myself, I had to sit down to keep from falling down. It was like hearing that someone in my family had died. It just didn't make any sense to me at all. My immediate response was to move home and take care of my dad. Not that he was incapacitated physically or anything, but just to be there for him. I felt so sorry for him.

Suzanne was in her last year of college, but she made arrangements to transfer to a campus closer to home so that she could live with her father. She told me that he was grateful to her for moving in with him but that he hadn't asked her to do so. It was her decision. An only child, Suzanne felt she was the only person her father could count on to help him through this crisis. "I just couldn't picture him getting along on his own," she said. "I had to be there for him." In fact, her father was going through the motions of his normal routine. He went to work and kept up with evening business meetings that he had to attend, but according to Suzanne, he was "in a daze."

> He'd come home from work or from a meeting and have this sad, dejected look on his face, like he was in a daze. My dad has never been an overly talkative person. He's a sweet man, very generous and kind but doesn't come out and tell you what he's feeling. Those first few months or so after my mom left, he opened up a little with me—enough to tell me how stunned he was that my mom had decided to end a twenty-five-year marriage that he'd thought was something she valued. When friends of theirs had gotten divorced, he said he'd been grateful that he and my mom were still so happy together. It was like my mother's affair and her decision to leave him had completely knocked the wind out of him.

The fact that her mother had been unfaithful and rejected her father made it even harder for Suzanne to separate herself from an increasingly dependent relationship with him:

> I know it sounds strange, but if my mom had died, I don't think I would have felt the same kind of sympathy for my dad. But his suffering was about feeling, not only lost without her, but terribly rejected. And it pulled at me. I felt so bad for him that I wanted to do whatever I could to cheer him up, to prove to him that he was loved.

Wanting to make up for the pain her mother had caused, Suzanne spent nearly all of her free time with her dad. She made him dinner almost every night and planned outings for the two of them on the weekends. Saturday nights they had a standing date to go out to dinner. Suzanne researched interesting new places to eat, restaurants that her mom and dad hadn't gone to together. When I asked her if her father had any friends that he could have turned to during that time, Suzanne said he wasn't up to being around his old friends given the humiliation he felt about his wife's betrayal.

Most of his friends were friends of my mother's, too, so he said he didn't fit in anymore. It wasn't just that he'd be the only single man with all these married couples; it was that he couldn't face them. The few times when he was invited to a dinner party or barbecue, he declined. He told me that it was too hard to be around their mutual friends. Then he would say something like, "I'm so lucky to have you, Suzanne" or "I don't know what I'd do without you, honey," and I'd get this queasy feeling inside. That's when I started realizing that maybe he was starting to depend on me too much. It was like I had become his stand-in partner.

When she initially moved in with him, Suzanne hadn't really thought about how long she would live with her dad, but after nearly a year, she realized that their routine together meant she had very little time for her own social life. She went to classes, studied in the library, occasionally had dinner with a friend, but that was it. She didn't go to parties like she had when she was away at school, and she didn't date. Her father had become her primary companion. Although it had been her idea to help her dad cope with the trauma of losing his wife to another man, Suzanne hadn't anticipated how dependent he would become. But now she felt uncomfortable telling him how she felt about his growing reliance on her. So she went to the counseling center on campus and saw a therapist who helped her get up the courage to approach her father:

The therapist helped me realize that I wasn't doing my father or me any good by spending all my free time with him. He had to get out there and make new friends, and I needed to get back to my life. I was twenty-one and I'd never had a serious boyfriend. I had to start thinking of myself. But it was hard. When I told my dad that I was planning to move back up north, I felt like I was breaking his heart. Of course, he said he understood and told me that I'd already sacrificed way too much, but I could tell he was not looking forward to being on his own. I had to steel myself to make the break.

It's not unusual for a child of infidelity to want to fill in the empty spaces in the life of a betrayed parent, especially if that parent is kind and undemanding and obviously in pain, as Suzanne's dad was. But her therapist was right in encouraging Suzanne to make a break from her dad. It wasn't healthy for either of them to become each other's partner; both needed the opportunity to have their own relationships. As it turned out, a few weeks before Suzanne left, her father finally accepted an invitation to a dinner party at which he met a recently divorced woman. They dated only a few times, but it gave him the courage to put himself out there socially for the first time since his separation from his wife.

Five years have passed since Suzanne first moved in with her father, and she now has a new perspective on how she rushed in to take care of him after that initial shocking phone call.

I think my father is a lot stronger, a lot more resilient than I gave him credit for. After I left, he missed me. He was lonely. But he took steps to meet someone. He joined a singles group and he stuck with it until he found a woman he really likes. They may even get married. I would have never, ever pictured my dad going to a singles group—but it turns out he adapted to a totally new situation.

I love my dad so much, and it was my instinct to rush off to protect him after my mom left. I didn't think twice about it. But now I think maybe he didn't need all that protecting.

Suzanne is the type of loving person who gives of herself when a loved one needs her, but perhaps she has a tendency to give too much. Not many adult children would have committed so much time to a betrayed parent in the way that Suzanne did. I'm sure that the love she gave to her father helped him to get through the crisis of infidelity, but was it necessary for Suzanne to spend so much time with him to give her dad the emotional support he needed? As her therapist pointed out, Suzanne's ongoing presence was not helping either father or daughter.

Suzanne had decided to move back home because she intuited her father's fragility when her mother left him for a lover. She perceived him as "lost" and couldn't picture him getting along on his own. Suzanne would never have imagined that her father could move on and make new friends, even become involved with a new partner. It's quite likely, however, that her father would have reached out to other people much sooner had Suzanne not been there for so long, fulfilling his emotional and social needs. It is clear that her dad had the ability to change his social habits, as evidenced by his joining the singles group once Suzanne left.

Many children of infidelity can't help but be involved in the initial turmoil when one parent discovers that the other has been unfaithful. And adult children can certainly provide some emotional support to a betrayed parent at first. But as the shock of discovery begins to diminish, children of any age need to get back to their own lives. For adult children, it may be necessary to comfort a parent and be there for him (or her) until the reality of what has happened sinks in and the parent begins to takes steps to reorient his life. However, children of infidelity need to continue with their own personal and social lives, and the betrayed parent needs to take charge of his own recovery from the crisis without relying on his children. It is inappropriate for children to become emotional caretakers for a parent; to the contrary, parents need to be emotionally available to the child or adult child, a task that is not easily performed during a time of crisis.

It appears that Suzanne felt she needed to take care of her father because she didn't trust that he could take care of himself. He had apparently been so dependent on his wife for his social and emotional needs that Suzanne felt he wouldn't be able to make it on his own. And as a woman, perhaps Suzanne felt guilty on behalf of her mother. She told me that it took her many months before she was ready to reconnect with her mom and to meet her mother's boyfriend. She still holds it against her mother for causing her father so much pain. But as he moves on with his new life and seems much happier, it is easier for Suzanne to let go of both the worried concern for her dad and the anger toward her mom. She has begun to see her parents in a new light, as people with identities that are separate from their roles as mother and father, husband and wife. Suzanne has also gained a new respect for her father, having witnessed how willing he has become to make significant changes in his life.

Molly's Story: "I had to escape my mom's dependence on me."

Like Suzanne, Molly became the emotional caretaker of her betrayed parent, but she took on the role far less willingly than Suzanne. In fact, when she was still in high school, Molly moved out of her home for two years in order to escape her mother's "clinging" tendencies. An affair between her father and his secretary, and his subsequent decision to move out, had left Molly's mother in a state of turmoil. With three children to care for and little financial support from her soon-to-be ex-husband, Molly's mom relied heavily on her teenage daughter. Molly increased her hours at an after-school job and also babysat her younger sister and brother, but as much as her mom counted on Molly for practical assistance, it was the emotional caretaking that took its toll on the fifteen-year-old.

Our lives fell apart. . . . I have a handicapped younger sister and a little brother who was only six at the time, so it was just chaotic. It was terrible—terrible, terrible, terrible in so many ways. My mother was very angry, of course. And hurt. And we didn't see our father. In some ways it was a blessing that we didn't see him. I didn't really want to see him. I was furious at him. And I certainly didn't want to know anything or have anything to do with his girlfriend. So it was just a really hard time.

Prior to the affair, Molly had always been "daddy's girl," while her mother's personality had often rubbed her the wrong way. She told me that her dad was "comforting to be with and very calm—a nice guy, never mean to anybody, jovial, and pretty fair-minded. You could get good advice from my dad, whereas my mother is more hysterical." If Molly knew her mother to be "hysterical" prior to the infidelity crisis, after her husband's betrayal, Molly's mom's frantic moods intensified. In addition to feeling overwhelmed by the financial and child-care burdens after her husband left, Molly's mother often became so distressed that her ability to be a good parent was severely hampered.

As too often happens in homes where parental infidelity leaves the betrayed parent feeling desperate and insecure, there were times when Molly had to become like a mother to her own mother. In describing this dynamic, Molly again referred to a time prior to the infidelity scenario, when she had preferred her father's company to her mother's:

My mother was so intense—she still is. She's clinging and overwhelming and very dependent on me for emotional support. She wants me with her all the time, which is the story of my whole life. This intensified when my dad left; he had really been the buffer. My preference had always been to be with him. I was his favorite, he was my favorite—we were buddies. But when he left, I had the full force of my mother to contend with. And I did a lot of parenting of her.

At the same time Molly was filling the role of parent to her mother, she was also coping with her own sense of devastation over the loss of the father who had once been her "buddy" (and a buffer between her and her mom). Molly was deeply angry at her father for running off with his secretary and for preferring a "trashy woman" and her young children over his real family. She also felt ashamed of how her father had transformed from a respectable man in the community to someone who abandoned his wife and children. His secretary girlfriend (who later became his wife) discouraged him from seeing his children, so Molly's dad essentially lost touch with Molly and her sister and brother.

Compounding her overwhelming sense of loss was the fact that her father's side of the family abandoned Molly and her siblings as well:

There was tremendous shame, just tremendous shame. It felt so humiliating that my dad took up with this trashy woman. Like, he chose that over us? And I was so angry that I told my grandparents, and I told them every little detail. Well, what happened then was they cut us off, too. They couldn't take it. They couldn't tolerate what was being said about their son. I think they didn't want to believe it. And so after that, I only ever saw those grandparents one more time. So I lost them, too.

Meanwhile, Molly's best friend's family became her saving grace. Craving the stability of an intact family—and parents who were able to nurture her rather than needing nurturing themselves—Molly reached out to her friend's family and allowed them to take her in.

As a teenager, I moved in with another family. I just didn't want to be in my family. My whole goal in life as a teenager was to get away from all of them. I went to live with my best friend's family. I would go home on the weekends, but I feel like her family really saved me. She had a wonderful dad and a mom who were totally the opposite of mine. They were perfect for me. It was such a relief to be away from all the chaos and tension, you know? So, God bless them for taking me in. I was there every night for two years.

It is understandable that Molly would want to escape from the sadness, anger, and chaos left behind when her father's infidelity led to his abandonment of the family. Leaving home was a healthy choice for her in the sense that it allowed her to distance herself from the family conflict, but in another sense she did what her father had done: leave. Children of infidelity whose cheating parent leaves the home are bound by two worlds—that of the betrayer who takes off, and that of the betrayed who is left behind. Either world feels uncomfortable, and the child is left with the feeling of being trapped. Molly felt trapped because even though she experienced a sense of relief being at her friend's house, she continued to worry about her betrayed mother. She went home on the weekends to be with her mom, and as an adult she continued to take care of her mother in various ways.

Molly couldn't prevent the emotional scars of parental infidelity. For years she chose older partners, perhaps in an attempt to replace the fathering she missed. And it took her a long while to deal with her anger toward her father and her resentment toward her mom, and to fully understand the repercussions of her family's upheaval. Molly feels fortunate to have found a therapist when she was in her twenties who helped her sort through the parental infidelity-related issues she was still struggling with. Even now, more than thirty years since her father's affair was first discovered, Molly still struggles with her relationship to her mom. She says that her mother continues to suffer over her ex-husband's betrayal. And Molly is still called upon to "be there" for her betrayed mom.

I think infidelity enrages the partner. It's such an enormous betrayal. My mother was wrecked, absolutely wrecked. I would say my mother never recovered. Probably to this day she's never recovered. So she was very compromised in her parenting of us. Plus the fact that she had to work very, very hard—and really lost her sense of self.

But the other thing that comes with that, of course, is that I think kids who are protecting the betrayed parent are doing it, but they don't really want to. At least that's how it was for me. I really protected my mother. I was even buying her clothes, making sure that she had fabulous birthdays and Christmases, and all of that. But I didn't really want to. I wanted to get away. It was a terrible ambivalence that I feel to this day.

Molly realizes that her mother is still overly dependent on her, but at this point she finds it difficult to abandon the role she has played for so long. Now that her mom is elderly, it is especially hard for Molly to insist that she take more responsibility for her own emotional well-being. The mother-daughter dynamic that began as a response to Molly's father's betrayal and abandonment continues to be a burden to Molly. When she speaks of a "terrible ambivalence" that is still with her, Molly is referring to the conflict between her resentment and the love and compassion she feels for her mom. It is a state of mind shared by other children of infidelity who find themselves cast in the unwelcome—and inappropriate—role of emotional caretaker to a betrayed parent.

Nicole's Story: "My mom punished us for my dad's affairs."

Nicole's father cheated on her mother throughout their long marriage, and yet Nicole's resentment has always been directed at her mom, not her dad. She faults her mother, not only for putting up with the infidelity and staying in the marriage, but for taking out her anger on Nicole and her siblings. While she acknowledges that her father's adultery instigated the animosity between her parents, Nicole blames her mother for the fallout: a chaotic, dysfunctional household. According to Nicole, because her mother allowed the infidelity to continue, she was not worthy of her daughter's respect.

The way the dynamic worked was that he cheated on her and she was just this really angry person, and she would take it out on us. They would be fighting all the time, she'd be like the devil, and she'd take it out on us kids because we were easier targets. Her parenting was terrible, and she was in such a bad marriage that we, the children, paid for it. Years later, she would say, "I stayed with him so you would have your father at home," but from about the age of nine or ten, I was a precocious kid, and I used to tell her, "Leave him!" I had very little respect for her. I think she liked being the victim, because someone does that to you once, twice, three, four times—but there's a point at which you gain some self-respect and try to move on with your life. So my anger about that whole thing was toward her, not him.

Nicole also spoke of her mother's poor self-image and of how it impressed her in a negative way as well. Because Nicole's mom didn't seem to value herself very highly, Nicole didn't either. Sadly, Nicole came to believe that her mother deserved to be cheated on:

My mom has always felt that my dad was better than her, smarter than her—better-looking, more charming, so I think she was willing to put up with anything he dished out. I know it sounds twisted, but I think I justified what he did because my mom had such low self-esteem that I believed her when she said that she was less than him. And so how could I blame him for wanting to be with other women—because she wasn't good enough. I kind of bought into her mentality about that.

While Nicole vented her anger at her mom for remaining with her adulterous dad, she didn't resent her father for telling her about his girlfriends. In fact, she adored her father and found the women he spoke about, who were so unlike her mother, to be "fascinating":

My dad would tell me these stories of his conquests of other women, and why he found this one attractive, or why this one was so wonderful. He made them sound really fascinating. And my mom was just this solid woman—he never said anything exciting about her to me. Obviously he loved her, because he didn't leave her. And when she would kick him out, he would beg and beg to stay. But I didn't see it that way, because I never understood why he loved her, or if he loved her—or why he was even with her in the first place. I didn't get that.

What Nicole did "get" was that her father loved her, even seemed to put her on a pedestal. She told me that his love and attention gave her a sense of self-assurance, so that Nicole came to see herself as everything her mother wasn't—strong, confident, and adored. The contrast between the way her father treated her mother and the way he treated Nicole couldn't have been more striking. And Nicole is well aware of that disparity:

> *My father was a horrible husband, but he was a great, great dad. And I really do think that he gave me a sense of confidence. He made me think that I was so wonderful, the apple of his eye, daddy's little girl. It's interesting because, as a kid, it set up a really weird family dynamic. My mom was jealous of our relationship. I think my dad sort of contrasted me with my mom, because I was very different from her.*

Perhaps in an unconscious effort to prove just how different she was from her unhappy mother, whose husband constantly cheated on her, as an adult Nicole sought out the role of "the other woman." At one point she was involved in an affair with a married man who would become the most important relationship in her life. Clearly, however, commitment and marriage were not on her agenda.

> *I used to have this thing where I was interested in men who were committed to other women. So I kind of wanted to be like "the other woman." My husband was married when I met him. So he had an affair—with me—and he left her. We're married now, and I think the process of us getting together was probably the most painful time in my life, because all these things came to a head. When we were getting more serious about our relationship—going from just having an affair to talking about him leaving his wife and marrying me—I had a hard time with that part of it. I thought, If I get married, what about all of this commitment stuff? And I had to kind of work through this idea of becoming someone's wife and what that meant.*

It's not hard to understand why Nicole wouldn't want to become someone's wife. From the time she was a little girl, being a wife signified to Nicole everything she detested in her mom—her anger and bitterness, her lack of self-esteem, her permanent status as a victim. Nicole perceived her mother as a long-suffering victim of infidelity who was not only miserably unhappy but who did nothing to either change her husband's behavior or extricate herself from a bad marriage—and who instead inflicted her misery on her children. In Nicole's mind, becoming the other woman, like the fascinating, independent characters her father described to her when she was younger, was a far more appealing role. And one she enjoyed for a number of years—until one of her affairs turned into a marriage.

When I asked Nicole how she would assess her current relationship with her mom, she told me that it hasn't changed that much, but her attitude toward her mother is slowly beginning to shift.

I'm developing more empathy for her but it's a slow process, a really slow process. I try to be more sensitive and understanding, and I definitely think that as I'm married longer I'm starting to understand how much more complicated marriage is, instead of standing outside it looking in. I try to be more understanding of my mom, but I still don't get it. I still don't get why she put up with my dad's affairs. I still don't get what she was thinking, because I'm definitely not that kind of wife that you cheat on.

Children aren't privy to the nuances of their parents' relationship, so it's more than likely that Nicole wasn't aware of the entire story behind her parents' unfaithful marriage. It is understandable why she preferred her father's charm to her mother's sourness, because while it is more common for a child of infidelity to sympathize with the betrayed parent, when that parent is harsh or bitter, as Nicole's mother was, it makes sense that a daughter or son would be turned off and harbor resentment. Nicole's father, on the other hand, appeared to her as someone who enjoyed his fascinating lifestyle and felt entitled to cheat on his wife. He also showered Nicole with loving attention.

Nicole took the lessons she gleaned from her childhood and initially made the choice to lead the sort of life that her father and his lovers seemed to enjoy. Rather than follow in her mother's footsteps by committing to a relationship that could lead to betrayal and misery, Nicole wanted to become the type of desirable woman that her father was attracted to. But as we all discover eventually, life is never a simple contrast between black and white. With time, Nicole is learning that her own happiness is not about being either the other woman or the married woman; rather, it is about feeling authentically herself in a relationship founded on love.

Ryan's Story: "I didn't like my mom painting my dad as the villain."

Children of infidelity are too often torn between allegiance toward one parent and empathy for the other. And sometimes when a betrayed parent tries to get a child to "side with" him or her by demonizing the betrayer, this attempt to elicit empathy can backfire. Such was the case with Ryan, who was eleven years old when his parents separated due to his father's affair. According to Ryan, who is now twenty-five, at first his sympathies were with his mom.

My dad met the woman who eventually became my stepmom because she's a hairdresser, so he would take me to get my hair cut. I don't know if that was his way of introducing me, or he was just trying to get to know her, but that kind of just bothered me afterward. At first, it was just like, okay I'm getting my hair cut from some lady my dad knows.

When I realized he was having an affair with this woman, I was like really upset. I just felt like my dad just kind of ruined everything. But I was still kind of left in the dark on everything, because I was so young. I don't think he thought I could understand everything, but . . . I remember once when my dad had already moved out and he had his own place, I was looking through his organizer-datebook, and he had something in there about his lover's birthday. And I remembered that my mother's birthday was in December. So that pissed me off, and I confronted my dad about it.

When Ryan confronted him, his dad said that he had made a mistake a few years earlier by cheating on Ryan's mom, which was the reason for their earlier separation. They had gotten back together again, but at that point Ryan's mom had told her husband that she loved him but was no longer "in love" with him. So Ryan's father felt he had the right to find someone else who could be "in love" with him—and that's why he began the affair with the hairdresser. Ryan's dad told his son that he felt he had the right to be happy.

Hearing his father's side of the story, Ryan felt more sympathetic toward him. He also told me that he had always looked up to his father, loved him very much, and resented the fact that his mother and aunt denigrated him in front of Ryan and his siblings.

I don't think my dad is such a villain, like maybe my mom makes him out to be. After she and my dad split up, she would take us with her when she would go to her friends' houses, and I remember very distinctly that my uncle's ex-wife, my aunt, was very negative about my father. She would be very vocal about it around me, every time. And that would really upset me, because when my dad was around, she was so fake and so friendly to him, and then when he was gone, she'd be just like bashing him—even calling him a pig. And I just thought that was really wrong. It's not even her place—just because she's friends with my mom, she doesn't have the right to put my father down, especially while I'm there.

Ryan's aunt and mother were clearly a united front in the bad-mouthing of his dad, and Ryan took it upon himself to defend the father he still deeply loved and admired:

When I'd hear my mom and aunt talking that way about my dad, I'd yell at them and say that they don't know anything about my father and they should keep their mouths shut. I didn't like it. I didn't like people trying to paint my dad in this light, because he's my father—and I know he loves me and he loves us. Whatever he did, it wasn't because he wanted to hurt my family or intentionally hurt my mom, you know? He's a man, and he's a person, and he's allowed to make mistakes in life.

Fourteen years after his parents' breakup, Ryan still expresses outrage that his father was "painted in a bad light." I think that his need to defend his father is quite common among children of infidelity who feel that their cheating parent is being unfairly characterized by the betrayed parent and other relatives. Not only did Ryan talk about the fact that "everyone makes mistakes" and that his father didn't intentionally hurt his family, but he also looks up to his dad as a strong, loving, charismatic man. Ryan made a point of telling me that his father is well liked by everyone (except his mom and his aunt) and that people are easily drawn to him. He clearly identifies with his father, stating that he thinks he and his dad have a lot in common—including being tempted by other women.

I'm an adult, too, now, and I have a girlfriend that I've been with for a long time, and I know what it's like to—you know. Especially when you're with somebody, it's when you have the confidence. Other women start giving you attention, which happens to me a lot, and only when I'm with my girlfriend do I get this attention, you know?

So that's how I see it. My dad is very confident, and he's a great person and everyone loves to be around him. I always want to emulate my dad, because I look up to him a lot. People are always telling me that I look like him and act like him, and everyone loves my dad. Even people in my mom's family, they're like, "oh, I saw your dad and said hi," and like, he just has a great personality. Who wouldn't be attracted to someone with a great personality?

So even my aunt (who puts him down) or all these people who talk crap about my father, now I look at it as them being jealous. My dad would do really nice things for my mom—on Mother's Day and stuff like that. So I just think my dad is a very good person, kind, and he is a romantic in a lot of ways. Those people don't see stuff like that—especially like my aunt.

While it may be difficult for a betrayed parent to keep her (or his) resentment under wraps, it is very important to do so when children are within earshot. Children of any age shouldn't have to hear harsh, disrespectful comments about their parent—even one who has been unfaithful. And they shouldn't be forced to buy into their betrayed parent's negative perspective on their other parent to prove their allegiance. As Ryan's story reveals, a cheating parent can also be a child's cherished role model, albeit one who makes mistakes. To label the unfaithful father or mother as a villain, not only robs the cheating spouse of his or her positive attributes, it also robs the child of his own perspective on one of the two most important people in his life.

Gail's Story: "My mother still holds it against me for wanting a relationship with my father."

When Gail's mother learned one afternoon that her husband was having an affair, she fell apart. Gail came home from high school to find her mom sitting on her bed in the dark, crying inconsolably to herself. A twenty-two-year marriage that Gail and her older brother had always thought was strong and stable was, in fact, shattered. Gail was shocked. How could this be happening to her perfectly normal family? At first she thought that she might be able to prevent her father from leaving and going off with the other woman:

> *I remember for a few months I thought I could maybe do something to help get them back together. This all happened at the culmination of my high school experience—I was cheerleader, class president, homecoming court. In fact, the day I found out that I had been chosen for homecoming court and that I might become homecoming queen was the same day I came home to this whole scene with my mom finding out about my dad's girlfriend and falling apart. But for a while I thought,* If I just win homecoming queen, maybe dad would be happy. *Very soon I realized that wasn't going to happen.*

After the affair was discovered, Gail's mother began talking about her husband in very derogatory terms. She also tried to enlist Gail's assistance in confronting him at his lover's apartment. Somewhat defensive on her father's behalf and definitely not wanting to become involved in any confrontational schemes, Gail was upset by her mother's behavior:

> *There was one incident where she was driving, she and I were in the car together, and she drove by an apartment where my father's car was parked outside, and she said, "That's where his girlfriend lives." And she said, "I want you to go to the door and ask for him." I refused, but it was just that kind of environment—very tense. I think my mother was desperate, and maybe for a little while she believed she could keep him or she wanted to go there and confront him, to shake some reality into him by saying, "Here's your daughter knocking on your girlfriend's door"—to shame him perhaps.*

Gail's parents got divorced and her father married the other woman, but their marriage lasted only about five or six years. Meanwhile, Gail's mother was never able to work through her bitterness toward her husband, and Gail says she expected her to feel the same antipathy toward her father. But Gail perceived her mother as someone who "allowed herself to be walked over."

Although Gail hadn't known about her father's unfaithfulness prior to that fateful afternoon when she found her mom crying on the bed, her mother had been aware of it earlier in their marriage. The fact that her mother had never taken steps to confront her husband's infidelity one way or another was something Gail held against her: " She told me that for years she knew what was going on, and yet she seemed to go along with it. When she was going through the breakup, there were times when I wanted to shake her and say, 'Grow a backbone!'"

Twenty-five years after the infidelity that caused the dissolution of her marriage, Gail's mom continues to condemn Gail for allegedly taking her father's side. Her evidence of this is that Gail has a warm relationship with her dad. In Gail's mother's eyes, Gail's desire to keep up a close connection to her father is proof that she is being disloyal to her mom. On the other hand, Gail's brother has distanced himself from their dad and thus, unlike Gail, has earned his mother's approval. All these years after the fact, Gail's mother still resents Gail for not giving her the emotional support she continues to need, and Gail is still angry and hurt by her mom's self-centered expectations:

My mother and I exchange letters and she brings up things from twenty-five years ago, as if it was yesterday. She obviously is not letting go of anything. She and I have continued to have a really troubled rela-

tionship, because I have a relationship with my father. She's encouraged my brother to distance himself from him, and my brother pretty much has. But I refused to take sides. My dad has always been supportive of me. He and his wife even helped me take care of my baby when I was breaking up my marriage, and I've always been very grateful for that. My mother was really angry about it, though.

Gail's mother also made it known that she doesn't approve of Gail's current partner, with whom Gail had a second child. Her mom went so far as to proclaim an ultimatum: it's either him or me. Reminiscent of her stance at the time of her breakup with Gail's father, she was asking Gail to choose sides. This time, the choice was just as unfair as it had been when Gail was a high school student refusing to spy on her father:

My mother told me that she took one look at my current partner and decided that he was going to be just like my father—that he would cheat on me, that he would lie to me. And she told me that I had to choose between my partner and her. I refused to do that. So she cut me off, stopped talking to me for many months. And then out of the blue she started talking to me again. But when I became pregnant a few years ago, she again stopped talking to me and hasn't talked to me since.

It became clear to me during our conversation that Gail feels deeply hurt by her mother's withdrawal. We talked about how her mom's behavior reflects the fact that she has failed to resolve the issues surrounding her husband's betrayal. She still needs Gail to be there for her, to be on her "side." Even though Gail has explained to her mom that being forced to choose between one's parents is never appropriate, and that even an unfaithful dad should be allowed to maintain close ties with his daughter, Gail's mom is unable to see their family dynamic in this way. In her mother's eyes, Gail is not only a traitor but also blind to the fact that Gail's partner is just like her father, a man who will cheat eventually. In a twisted sort of logic, Gail's love for her partner communicates to Gail's mother that Gail believes it is okay for a man to be like her dad.

Sadly, the emotional battering that Gail's mom continues to inflict upon her daughter stems from Gail's simple desire to have her father in her life. As Gail so plainly put it, "I still want him to be my parent." Gail needs to tell her mother why maintaining a relationship with her father is necessary for her, and that their relationship has nothing to do with his unfaithfulness in the marriage. Gail also needs to explain to her mom that the connection Gail has with her dad does not take away from her love for her. As for Gail's mother's attempt to make Gail choose between her partner and her, it may be that she has legitimate concerns about Gail's partner's trustworthiness; still, her role as a mother is to express her concerns and then step back and allow Gail to make her own decisions.

It appears that Gail's mother may not be ready to respect the boundaries between a parent and an adult child. If this is the case, then Gail will need to understand that her mother is incapable of accepting that Gail has a right to her own life. At some point, Gail's mother may realize that her daughter loves her and that there is no need to hurt her by giving her the silent treatment. Until that time, Gail will need to make peace with her mother's inflexibility, while still leaving room for the possibility of a better relationship with her at some point down the road.

DEALING WITH A CHILD'S SYMPATHY FOR OR RESENTMENT TOWARD THE BETRAYED PARENT: ADVICE FOR PARENTS

- It is common for the betrayed spouse and children to stick together during the initial phase of the infidelity crisis. Once that time has passed, however, children need to relate to their own support system—friends, extended family, and their own spouses if they're already married—and parents have to find their own answers independently from their children.

- If necessary, parents and children can each benefit from psychological counseling during the crisis period. It is never the children's responsibility—regardless of their age—to take care of their parents emotionally.

- Parents should always remember that the relationship between husband and wife is very different than that between parent and child. Children of every age need to maintain a positive connection with their parent, even if that parent is the "guilty party" in an infidelity scenario.

- Never encourage your child to "take sides" or to feel animosity toward his or her cheating parent—even though you may feel it yourself.

- If you need to vent your feelings of anger and hostility toward your unfaithful spouse, do so with a trusted friend or therapist, not in the presence of your children.

DEALING WITH SYMPATHY FOR OR RESENTMENT TOWARD YOUR BETRAYED PARENT: ADVICE FOR OLDER CHILDREN AND ADULT CHILDREN OF INFIDELITY

- If you are tempted to hold your betrayed parent responsible for the other parent's unfaithfulness, remember that you do not know the whole story behind your parents' marriage or what may have led to the infidelity that occurred within it. There are always influences and issues that a child of infidelity is unaware of. With the exception of a professional counselor or therapist, your parents are the only ones who can accurately assess their relationship.

- Trust that your betrayed parent can survive the infidelity crisis without your ongoing emotional support. Allow your father or mother to get through this on his/her own or with the help of a trusted friend or a qualified professional, if needed. If you feel that it is warranted, you can be sympathetic and comforting toward your betrayed parent, but be aware that an appropriate emotional boundary should always exist between a parent and child, regardless of the child's age.

- If you are holding on to resentment toward your betrayed parent for depending on you for emotional support, for criticizing your other parent in front of you, or for neglecting you throughout his or her infidelity crisis, try to accept that none of us receives ideal parenting. Your betrayed parent likely experienced considerable pain, sadness, and anger, which may have resulted in their being incapable of being the parent you needed them to be. It is never too late to work through your resentment, and when you do so effectively, you'll be able to let go of it. The exercises at the end of Chapter 8 are an excellent way to begin that process.

SEVEN

Am I Acting Out My Parents' Infidelity Drama?

She was definitely upset about her mother's affair, but I never thought it would lead to this.

—*Father of fifteen-year-old Rona, referring to his daughter's drug use and self-abuse*

My father always had other women, so I just kind of thought it was normal. When I grew up, I would always be involved with men who were in relationships. And I remember making that almost a conscious thought, like, "Okay, guys cheat; it's gonna happen anyway, and it's better to be the other woman than the girlfriend or the wife or whatever," and that's kind of how I used to live my life.

—*Female survey respondent, age forty-three*

I enjoy anonymous sex more than intimacy. I'm always looking for the "next thing" and not appreciating the person in front of me.

—*Male survey respondent in his thirties, referring to how he has been affected by his father's infidelity*

When children are unable to deal with the confusion, shame, anger, and resentment that arise from a family's infidelity scenario, they very often act out their painful emotions. A young child may withdraw socially, have temper tantrums, or engage in other disruptive behavior. An older child of infidelity may become involved in substance abuse, sexual promiscuity, or other self-destructive behavior as a way to bury the hurt or demonstrate unacknowledged feelings about their parent's actions. Rather than confront the distasteful, often shocking reality that one of their parents sexually cheated on the other, children may distract themselves with unhealthy, self-abusive activities. If they identify with the betrayer, they may feel that lies are okay if you are pursuing an activity or a relationship you enjoy—and that it's just a matter of not getting caught and learning how to cheat effectively. If their sympathies lie with the betrayed parent, older children and adult children may become victims of infidelity themselves, or they may choose partners with whom they can be the betrayer and thus act out a kind of revenge against their cheating parent.

In this chapter we'll hear from children of infidelity who suffered from the hurt and trauma of parental adultery and who processed their unresolved feelings by acting them out. Within each story and at the end of the chapter, I offer guidance for those of you who are parents dealing with children who are acting out, as well as those of you who are adults trying to understand your own behavior in the context of your parents' infidelity drama.

Rona's Story: "My mother acted like a tramp— so I guess that's what I am, too."

When fifteen-year-old Rona initially came to see me, it was her mom who brought her in. She had told me on the phone that Rona was having problems at school, her grades were slipping, and most days she didn't even want to go to class. Once in the office, however, Rona's mother refused to come into the session, insisting on staying in the waiting room.

Tall, attractive, and neatly dressed, Rona was clearly suffering, and it soon became clear that she had problems she couldn't share with anyone else. She complained of being depressed and said that it mainly had to do with what was going on at home. She told me that her parents were fighting a lot, and that it was making her so upset she could barely concentrate on anything else. She couldn't do her homework, she didn't want to hang out with her friends like she used to, and she didn't even feel like going to swim practice—her favorite activity. When I asked why her parents were fighting so much, Rona looked at me, not knowing if it was all right to tell me. She was guarded, and it wasn't until our next session together that the full story came out.

When Rona arrived the following week, her mother wasn't with her. Her father had brought her this time. Rona was still somewhat withdrawn and apprehensive, yet it was obvious that she wanted to share her story with someone. She had been using the computer and had opened the "deleted e-mail" file to discover e-mails from her mother to another man. Reading the e-mails, Rona pieced together her mother's hidden life. Her mom had met someone through the Internet and was having a relationship with him. Every few weeks, when Rona's mom had told her family she was going up north to visit her sister, she had actually gone to visit this man. Rona was devastated.

She told her father about what she had discovered, he confronted his wife, and Rona's parents had a horrible fight in which her mother threatened to leave home and go to live with the new man in her life. Her parents' arguments escalated, and after a few days Rona's mom left. She stayed with Rona's grandmother temporarily but soon after took off to live with the man she'd met on the Internet.

Rona thought her mother would come back, but she never did. Over the months that I continued to see her, Rona repeatedly referred to her mother as a whore. She told me she not only hated her mom but her mom's entire family as well—uncles, aunts, everybody. Everyone, that is, except her maternal grandmother, who was as critical of Rona's mother as Rona was. When she visited her grandmother, the two of them would talk about what a "tramp" Rona's mother was, and how awful it was that she had abandoned her children. Rona's mother tried to stay in touch, but when she phoned to try and speak with her daughter, Rona refused to talk to her.

Rona's problems grew as she now was responsible for her two younger brothers, and her inability to cope with so many emotional stresses and practical responsibilities gave way to a downward spiral. Discovering the truth about her mom's infidelity, having to be the one to tell her father about it, being left by her mother, and then having to take over the mothering role—all of this left Rona shocked, angry, overwhelmed, guilty, and in a tremendous amount of pain. Rather than feel the full extent of her emotional pain, Rona attempted to deflect it by hurting herself physically. She began cutting herself— her legs, arms, and abdomen. Rona was placed on an antidepressant medication, but she also started using marijuana and alcohol. And because she had gained a lot of weight on the medication she was taking for her depression, she started taking amphetamines so she wouldn't eat. Or she would attempt to starve herself. Whereas she had previously been on the swim team, she had now gained so much weight that she no longer qualified to be on the team.

Due to her increasing self-destructiveness, Rona exposed herself to dangerous situations and suffered the consequences. She and a few girlfriends would go to the beach at night and meet guys who would then take her and her friends to their apartment. To feel loved and accepted, Rona was willing to take risks. She was willing to go to a strange guy's apartment and to take drugs with him. She wanted a boyfriend, but she was unaware that these boys were not interested in a relationship. And due to her neediness and lack of self-value, she didn't know how to say no, to say "stop" when their physical affection escalated to having sex. So these encounters ultimately ended in date rape, as most of the time Rona was under the influence and unaware of what was going on. Rona didn't value her own sexuality, didn't value herself as a woman. She felt that being a woman was being trash—which was what she felt like when she let boys exploit her.

I don't want to imply that what happened to Rona was entirely the result of her mother's affair and Rona's estrangement from her. Rona had her own personality problems prior to these traumatic incidents. However, those problems were greatly exacerbated by her mother's actions. And Rona's self-destructive sexual behavior was definitely related to her feelings about being unloved by a mother who had become a "tramp." I can't say for certain that if Rona's mother hadn't had the affair, Rona would have chosen to be involved in healthier relationships. Given that she had a mother who was terribly dissatisfied with her life, Rona would probably still have had a hard time developing a confident sense of herself, but I doubt she would have gone through the turmoil she went through had her mother's affair not set off the chain of events that it did.

Rona witnessed the hardships her father had to go through by no longer having a wife to help nurture, raise, and provide for the children. And she found it hard to think of her mother as anything less than "a bitch" for having betrayed her husband and kids. She considered her mom a tramp and a deceiver, and she learned from her that women too easily fall out of love with their mate and in love with a guy simply because he tells her nice things—like the "nice things," her mother's boyfriend had written on the Internet. But Rona wanted to be told "nice things," too, and she craved love and affection even more once her mother left home. She valued herself so little that any guy was okay, as long as he paid her the slightest compliment. Of course, the guys she encountered perceived this longing in Rona and took advantage of her. They had sex with her and then left her, thus aggravating her emotional injury.

Given all she'd been through, Rona had a long way to go to work out what it means to be a woman, how to develop self-respect, and how to have a healthy relationship through mutual caring and trust. Before she could become involved with a young man, she needed to learn how to make decisions based on her emotional needs rather than acting out based on her mother's experience. If she didn't want to repeat the kind of abusive encounters she'd already had, she would have to give herself time to find out who she was and to value that person. She also had to learn to stop blaming herself for the breakup of her parents' marriage and for her mother's disconnection from the family.

Having been the one to divulge the secret of her mother's infidelity, Rona felt guilty and confused about her responsibility for the traumatic events that followed. It took her a long time to put everything in the right perspective and to realize that her mother's decision to have an affair and leave the family was not her fault. Rona can now acknowledge that, while the unhappy events following her mother's affair will always be part of her personal history, they don't have to harmfully affect her or her relationships from this point forward.

Frank's Story: "Am I punishing my mother for her affairs?"

When Frank came to see me, he was forty-one and facing his second divorce. During our sessions, he confronted the lies, suspicions, betrayal, and revenge that had plagued him since he was eight years old. As a boy, Frank had watched his uncles flirt with women at neighborhood parties and in the streets of their urban community. Although he felt "disgusted" by their behavior, it was considered normal in his culture for married men to have casual relationships with other women. Frank grew up in a culture that validated macho values; his married uncles role-modeled infidelity while his aunts complained about it but stood by their husbands. In Frank's case, however, it was not his father who was the cheater:

> *My dad was a wimp! I say this because I remember as a little kid being at a party, and my mom was dancing too close with another man. Everybody was looking at her and whispering about it. My dad did nothing, and I was very upset. Men in our family had mistresses—that was expected, and all my uncles were very open about it. I was disgusted by my uncles, but I learned that was the way it was for men. But women acting that way? No, that was an insult to our whole family.*

Frank discovered that his mother was indeed having an affair with the man she had been dancing with at the party. He had such a strong reaction to his mother's infidelity and his father's "wimpiness" that even at such a young age he felt his masculinity was being trampled on. Coming from a macho culture, it was no wonder that Frank was ashamed of his father for allowing his mother to get away with her flirtations and affairs. A woman should never be allowed to humiliate her husband like that, Frank told me.

So what kind of woman did Frank eventually choose to marry? A beautiful but flirtatious one with whom he could act out the infidelity drama and hopefully affirm what his father could not—an identity as a strong, macho male who knew how to deal with an unfaithful woman:

> *When I married at the age of twenty-four, I was very much in love. My wife was beautiful, but maybe too beautiful. I'll admit I liked how other men looked enviously at me, but I didn't like that she seemed to crave the attention. The turning point came when I walked in on her in the bedroom at a party we were at, kissing another man. It was coincidental that my rage was touched off again at a party, just as I had experienced as a little boy with my mom. Anyway, I loved my wife too much to divorce her, but after that I made her life miserable. And our young son's life, too.*

Frank paid his wife back for her flirtatiousness by having a number of extramarital affairs, which he never actually admitted to. He was indiscreet enough so that she always had doubts about what was going on, but he never confirmed her suspicions. Instead, he punished her by engaging in a painful emotional game that she could never fully figure out. Was he really staying late at the hospital where he held a powerful position as chief of staff, or was he carrying on with one of the pretty new nurses? There were always innuendos and suspicions, but no proof.

In fact, Frank had feelings for some of the women he slept with, but the relationships never lasted long enough to develop into anything beyond a brief sexual affair. As soon as one of his lovers would ask for more of a commitment, he would break it off. After years of his wife's unconfirmed accusations, and Frank emotionally battering her with vicious counter-recriminations and name-calling, she couldn't tolerate anymore and asked for a divorce. Frank still refers to his first wife as "the love of my life" and told me he doesn't really blame her for throwing him out—as if he expected that outcome all along.

Never having resolved the anger and hurt he felt toward his mother (for cheating and humiliating his father and the family), and toward his father (for not acting like a man), Frank went on to become unfaithful himself. His affairs were a way to prove his masculinity and his control over women who might behave as his mother had. When his wife betrayed him by being a flirt, Frank punished her with his many affairs, rather than confronting her in a more straightforward way. Had he and his first wife sought professional counseling, they might have realized why Frank's reaction to her behavior was so emotionally charged.

Sadly, Frank's family's infidelity became a chain reaction of infidelities. It's possible that his mother's betrayal had been a reaction to the macho society in which she was raised. But it nonetheless led to Frank's painful rage, which perhaps was the reason he chose a woman whom he knew might betray him—and with whom he could vent and thus tame that rage. When his wife gave him a reason to doubt her faithfulness, Frank got back at her by doing the very things for which he had always criticized his uncles.

But Frank's story doesn't end there. After his divorce from his first wife, he met someone else whom he eventually married—and with whom he continued to act out this family's infidelity saga.

When I was in my early thirties, I met this wonderful woman who loved me very much. I needed to know that she was going to be faithful to me, so I took my time to reassure myself that she would really be there only for me. I questioned myself, too. Could I be loyal to her and give up the cheating? I wasn't sure, but I promised myself I would try my best to be a loyal husband.

We married and had a son. But it was hard for me to say no to the women who came my way. Because of my prominent position at the hospital, women are attracted to what they perceive as power. At one point when my wife was pregnant, I didn't find her as attractive as she had been before, and this other woman insisted on having a relationship with me, knowing that I was a married man. I made a kind of bargain with myself. I decided that I could be loyal to my wife and stay in the marriage—while at the same time having an affair. Many of my male friends carried on in this way, so why couldn't I? I knew I was being unfaithful, but I felt that I was still committed to the marriage and our child. There was no way I would ever leave them.

It's interesting that Frank made a distinction between being sexually faithful and being committed to his marriage and family. He could agree to the latter, but not the former. This way of thinking reflected the same value system in which Frank had been raised. Although his father was never unfaithful, his mother and his uncles were. And his uncles always insisted that they were still being "loyal" to their wives and "committed" to their families even when they paraded their mistresses around the community.

Frank's affair lasted long enough for his wife to finally discover it. So he decided to end his relationship with the other woman, but he didn't find it easy. And it took a long time for his wife to recover from the betrayal and trust him again. They saw a marriage counselor, and Frank says he tried his best to meet his wife's expectations of fidelity, but he claims that, "my environment was always tempting me to do the opposite." After remaining faithful for a few years, Frank again gave in to a temptation that he says he simply couldn't turn away from.

Now, I feel very ashamed because I did it again! I thought about it, I remembered how much pain I had caused—to both of my wives. But I could not stop it! My wife found out, and, of course, she asked me for a divorce. Now I am about to lose my wife, who I love very much; the respect of my older son for the second time; and my own self-respect. And who knows how this is going to affect my younger son in the future?

Frank and I discussed the effects of his first marriage on his oldest son. Growing up with the knowledge of his father's infidelities, and witnessing his parents' constant allegations and counter-allegations, the boy never had the benefit of learning that it was possible to trust your spouse. Frank told me that his older son, who is now seventeen, had for years angrily lashed out at him for betraying his mother and has never had a close relationship with Frank. Frank doesn't want to create that same distance with his younger son but worries that the pattern of infidelity that he can't seem to undo will result in a similar rift.

Why did Frank's experiences as a child of infidelity necessarily result in his ongoing pattern of cheating on his wives? Although he knew intellectually that his mother's betrayal of his father had affected him, Frank never confronted himself on an emotional level to the point where he could clearly see the connection between his outrage as a child and his acting out that outrage with the women in his life. It took a second divorce and the loss of two women he deeply loved for Frank to want to begin to look at the impact his early exposure to infidelity has had. He is now beginning to examine the issues that led him to having affairs, instead of avoiding them by acting them out.

When people are unfaithful, in most cases it's not with the intention to hurt their partner or to break up the marriage, but rather to fill some personal need. Frank had the need to prove his manliness, to triumph over his mother's betrayal of his father. If he had been aware that his childhood experiences were what were motivating him, would that have been enough to stop him from having affairs? I can't say for sure, but it certainly would have made him stop and think before he acted on his temptation to cheat.

Also, if Frank had been conscious of the consequences of his actions, if he had taken care to weigh the pros and cons of infidelity, that may have helped him to end the cycle before his divorces. He might have posed these questions to himself: What does it mean to be a man? Can I trust women? Is it possible to have a monogamous relationship? Can I detach from the role models I witnessed in my younger years and develop my own? Do I have to remain emotionally distant from women out of fear that they may cheat on me? Can I confront my fears instead of acting on them? Can I stop punishing women as I would have liked my father to punish my mom?

Frank is now facing up to his history of infidelity—the chapter he inherited from his parents and the one he wrote himself. Now that he is challenging himself to become more conscious of what motivates his behavior, he has the chance to finally free himself from making the same self-destructive choices.

Lynn's story: "I felt entitled to cheat—just like my dad."

Like several other children of infidelity whose stories we've heard, Lynn considered her father "a horrible husband, but a good dad." She described him as "a good provider," the core quality by which fathers were judged in the 1960s when Lynn was growing up. "He wasn't a perfect dad—I'm not saying that at all—but he did the best that he could," Lynn told me. In other words, he was someone who tried to live up to what was expected of him as a family man. As for his standing as a husband, Lynn said that her mom was constantly hurling accusations of infidelity at her father. "Other women, other women, other women . . . when I was eight, nine, ten years old and my siblings were much younger, I remember those accusations and my parents' heated arguments."

One accusation, which was at least partially confirmed by Lynn when she was around nine or ten, involved her mother's younger sister, Lynn's aunt:

> *I remember my father showing a great deal of interest in one of my mother's younger sisters, who at that point must have been about twenty-five. She lived with our grandmother a couple of blocks away, and on Sunday outings, we would go and pick her up. My dad would beep the horn and tell us, "Wait here, I'll go and get her," and then he'd park and leave us kids and my mom in the car. After a while my mom would say, "Go and find out what's taking them so long." So I'd go into my grandma's house, and on two different occasions I saw him hugging my aunt from the back. I'd see through the door that he was hugging her and kissing her on the neck. I carried that image for a long time. That image is still so clear in my head.*

Other infidelity-related scenes from her childhood still stick in Lynn's mind as well: her mom throwing a Christmas tree across the room at her dad as she accused him of being out with another woman, coming home from school to find her mother physically assaulting a woman whom she claimed had been with Lynn's father, and numerous screaming fights her parents got into over her father's adulterous flings. Lynn says that her mom often told her she only stayed with her dad because of the children, but Lynn believes otherwise. Not only would her mother have been unable to make it on her own economically, but, according to Lynn,

> *She really did not want to leave him. She loved him very, very, very much. . . . My mom would cry that she wanted a divorce. But then she would say, "How would I ever find somebody to take care of us?" and then the crisis [about his affairs] would just blow over, and she'd be happy again until the next blowup. But I know that she loved him. I know she did.*

When I asked her how her father's affairs and her mother's angry accusations affected her own relationships, Lynn began by telling me that she had spent her twenties, thirties, and early forties involved with a series of men, and that she had been unfaithful to all of them:

> *I either dated people who were like my father—handsome, life-of-the-party, screw everybody he wanted to—or then I dated for a long time men who were completely emotionally unavailable—again, like my father. And throughout every relationship that I had, all the way up to the last one before I got married [for the first time at age forty-five], I cheated on them. Every one of them. Some of it was minor cheating, if there is such a thing, and some of it was major.*

Lynn elaborated on the fact that in the course of all her serious relationships, she would take every opportunity to have secret sexual encounters with someone else. In one instance, when a live-in boyfriend was out of town, she flew off to be with a man she had recently met on a business trip. During another relationship that lasted five years, she would go out with other guys whenever her boyfriend was away. Such clandestine liaisons, Lynn confessed, are "a big part of my story."

When I asked her why she thought she had always cheated on her boyfriends, she told me that she wasn't seeking fun or excitement as much as she felt she was "entitled to it," since she was "holding my own, paying my rent, paying my own bills." It seems that in Lynn's mind, infidelity is closely associated with financial power. Her father paid all the bills, so he was entitled to do as he pleased, unlike her mother.

Lynn then talked about a particular time in her life when she justified her infidelity by virtue of the fact that she was supporting the man with whom she was living:

> *I was taking care of him, because he wanted to write a novel. I really cared about him, and I said, "Sure, I'll take care of you," but then I felt I could do whatever I wanted, and I did. It wasn't all the time; it was whenever I had the opportunity, though. And I chose to do it.*

Even if she wasn't financially supporting a boyfriend, in Lynn's mind her ability to provide for herself economically and not be dependent on a man (as her mother had been) meant that she was entitled to do whatever she wanted, including having affairs (as her father had).

Once Lynn got married, she seemed to turn a corner by making the decision to be faithful in her marriage. She had waited a long time to feel deserving of someone who wanted to commit to a permanent relationship with her, and she wanted to honor that commitment. However, at the very end of our interview Lynn revealed a secret that made it clear she is not entirely finished "acting out" in response to her parents' infidelity story:

> *I don't share with my husband the fact that I have had lunch with my ex-boyfriend two or three times. I have no interest at all in him, none*

whatsoever. And I really mean that. I'm not lying to myself. I'm not trying to hide anything at all. I love my husband so much; he's such a great guy, and we're really good friends, too, we are. But with my ex-boyfriend, it was a different kind of relationship. I miss the conversations that we had, I miss that intellectual stimulation, but I don't miss him. I would never go back to that. And I would never leave this wonderful human being who I'm married to for anything. I do really mean that. But it does concern me that I haven't told my husband.

Although Lynn is not technically cheating, she seemed unable either to say no to the secret lunches with her ex-boyfriend or to level with her husband about the lunch dates. She says that at one point she was on the verge of telling her husband about getting together with her ex-boyfriend just as friends, but she lost her nerve.

I almost told my husband about a year ago that I was going to have lunch with my ex-boyfriend. I said, "Would it really bother you if I had lunch with him?" and he said, "Well, why do you think you need to?" and I said, "I don't really need to, I just wonder about him sometimes." I was honest—as honest as I could be. I said, "I think about his family. I was really good friends with his sister." And my husband said, "Well, I don't know." We didn't resolve it, and we never brought it up again, so I just did it anyway. Because, to me, I don't feel that it's anything more than me having lunch with a friend, but I still don't want to tell my husband.

When Lynn asked me what I thought about her keeping this secret from her husband, I told her that I think secrets create a distance between partners because they force you to lie. Lynn had to lie to her husband when she had lunch with her ex-boyfriend; instead of being open and telling him the truth, she probably had to tell him that she had lunch with someone else—and then make up a story about a lunch that never took place. Granted, a lunch date is a far cry from sleeping with someone, but Lynn's need to keep the dates a secret invests them with an added significance. Secrecy inhibits trust in a relationship, and the more meaningful the secret, the greater the distance separating a couple. I told Lynn that her secret is a relatively minor one; however, her clandestine meetings with her ex-boyfriend actually constitute a mini-affair—an emotional affair. It's not just that she is seeking a type of communication with her ex-boyfriend that she is not pursuing with her husband; she is also lying to her husband about it.

How does this relate back to Lynn's parents' infidelity story? It seems to me that the secrets and lies surrounding the lunch dates are aspects of the acting-out behavior that Lynn has been engaging in for the last three decades. Ever since she has been old enough to have relationships with men, she has been behaving in response to the feelings she had about her father being a cheater and her mother being a victim. Lynn wanted to avoid being a victim of infidelity, so she avoided marriage and made sure she was never in a fully committed relationship. When she was involved with a boyfriend, she became the cheater to protect herself from becoming the victim. Once she got married, the stakes were raised because of the explicit vow to be faithful. Perhaps Lynn's emotional affair is her attempt to have it both ways—the control in knowing that she is the cheater and not the victim, without the actual breaking of her marriage vow and the consequences of a sexual affair.

Lynn seemed to want to convince herself that she is not harming her marriage by having lunch with her ex-boyfriend. Still, when I suggested that she might be engaging in an emotional affair, she concurred. And it sounds as if she's still not sure that she can give up that last vestige of acting out, which her lunch dates represent:

I understand what you mean by that emotional stuff, I really do. Because whenever I see my ex-boyfriend, we have a fun time. We do. But for me, I do it over lunch. I don't make it drinks. I always tell him, "I have to leave by 12:30. I have to be out of here, I have another appointment." And we both really respect that. So we're not lingering. It's just. . . . Anyway, I guess I should just tell my husband that I don't mind doing this and that I hope it doesn't bother him. But if he said that it does bother him, then I'd have to make a decision, I guess.

What will it take for Lynn to make the decision to abandon her mini-affair and level with her husband? First of all, I think Lynn needs to realize that her secret relationship—even though it only consists of lunch dates—is a remnant of her previous "acting out" behavior. By continuing to engage in a clandestine relationship, she is demonstrating that she still needs to be unfaithful to avoid becoming a victim of infidelity. She justifies her "lunch-only" affair because it is not sexual, but she admits that she has an emotional connection to her ex.

More important, by lying about the get-togethers, Lynn may be setting herself up for more lies, which could seriously endanger her marriage. Hopefully, Lynn can come to realize that she does not need to have affairs to protect herself from getting hurt. Instead, she can find pleasure in an open and trusting relationship, with nothing to hide. And she can find excitement in the marriage itself, rather than in secrets that jeopardize that marriage.

Anthony's Story: "My mother's lover was my role model."

Anthony grew up in a home where his parents often argued about his father's alleged affairs. In fact, he remembers feeling grateful as a child when he came down with bronchitis because it provided a respite, forcing his parents to concentrate on his health rather than bicker at each other. Anthony never saw his father with another woman, but he did come into close contact with someone else who was instrumental in shaping Anthony's adult behavior: the man whom Anthony is certain was his mother's secret lover. Although he has only recently become aware of the extent to which his mother's infidelity has influenced his adult relationships, Anthony is beginning to realize that his own romantic choices and predilections are loosely modeled after those of the gentleman who was his mother's secret boyfriend.

Anthony claims to have freely chosen to be "the other man" in a series of love triangles, but might he actually be acting out the infidelity drama that he witnessed as a young boy? Acting out is never a behavior one freely chooses. Rather, we engage in acting-out behavior when we are unconsciously grappling with unresolved issues. This is how Anthony described how the drama of infidelity first appeared to him as a child.

> *I was pretty young, I'm not even sure how old, but my mother had a friend who would come over and visit her. In some way, I knew that they had a kind of relationship, and yet there was nothing I saw that would prove my mother was unfaithful. But this man would come and be with her and would never come over when my father was there. Even at that young age, I was suspicious. I remember asking my mother, "What is this man doing here in my house?"*

The only answer Anthony received from his mother was that the man was her friend and she enjoyed his company.

As an adult, Anthony was involved with a woman in a committed relationship for thirteen years; ten years living together and three years being married to her. He says they were faithful to each other throughout the relationship and that he married her, in part, to please his father who was dying and who wanted to see Anthony settled down. Anthony's father conveyed to his son that he was glad he hadn't become cynical about relationships given his mother's history of adultery.

Anthony agreed to marry his long-term girlfriend, with the stipulation that she not "manipulate" him into having a child. He was adamantly opposed to having children, because he claimed a child would interfere with the couple's relationship. When his wife became pregnant and wanted to keep the child, Anthony felt she had betrayed her promise. She ended up having an abortion, and the couple divorced.

Since then, Anthony has been drawn to relationships in which there is little chance of getting too close emotionally. He has been involved in three affairs with married women, and when I asked if he considered that he might be hurting these women's relationships, Anthony replied that he felt he was blameless.

Sometimes love gets lost within a marriage, and these women wanted love, or at least they desired sex. I never felt responsible for causing any of these women's relationships to end in divorce. I would never want to have that guilty feeling of having caused a rift in someone else's relationship.

Anthony rationalizes his affairs by offering some of the reasons others often use to defend infidelity. He claims that since human beings now live longer, people can't be expected to feel the same degree of love for each other throughout their lives. "The fire of the relationship goes out," he says, "and so you find that fire in somebody else." Perhaps Anthony's mother felt the diminishing of that fire in her marriage. Whether or not Anthony was aware of such things then, he now justifies the behavior of the married women with whom he has affairs, saying they are not to be blamed for their desires. Anthony's therapist recently told him that his special connection with his mother led him to refrain from judging her adversely, and to instead justify her behavior and that of other women who cheat on their husbands.

According to Anthony's perspective as "the other man," affairs are emotionally safe, whereas committed relationships are emotionally risky. It seems that after his long-term relationship fell apart, Anthony began to replicate the lifestyle of his mother's "visitor." Anthony is now beginning to understand that his role as "the other man" can be linked to his having witnessed his mother's relationship with her secret boyfriend. He told me that, "If I had to identify with someone, I would identify with him because I am also a free man, but a lonely man. He had a huge influence on me, even though I didn't know that when I was a child." While claiming that he feels "free and comfortable" being the third person in a relationship, Anthony admits that he feels more comfortable being the third person in a triangle than being betrayed himself.

While he acts out the role of the lover, which he learned from his mother's secret boyfriend, Anthony doesn't yet perceive that his penchant for this role may be evidence of his distrust for women. His ex-wife proved untrustworthy in his eyes because she had promised him she didn't want a child and then went back on that promise, thereby proving that she wanted a child more than she wanted him. "A child would have only intruded on our intimacy," Anthony says.

Anthony told me that he now sets limits for how intense a relationship should get. A love affair is fine, but he becomes very uncomfortable if that relationship progresses beyond being lovers. "I am not interested in being boyfriend and girlfriend," he says.

Although Anthony has undergone several years of therapy and

has some understanding of his motives, he is still acting out the repercussions of his family history, central to which was his mother's infidelity. He is still making decisions based on the unresolved feelings he had as a child. Rather than fully coming to terms with the anger, vulnerability, sadness, and lack of trust that his parents' infidelity drama instigated, Anthony is still acting out those deeply held emotions.

CHILDREN OF INFIDELITY WHO "ACT OUT": ADVICE FOR PARENTS

Betrayed and unfaithful parents alike usually lose their credibility with their children, as well as their authority. This can open the door to kids acting out their anger, confusion, and hurt. What can parents do to open the lines of communication with their children to help them face the painful truth about how parental infidelity is affecting them? Here are some core guidelines:

- The unfaithful parent must admit his or her wrongdoing and commit to not lying in the future if they are ever to win back some of the respect from their children. This in turn will encourage kids to face their parent's infidelity and to talk about how they feel about it.
- Parents should understand that a young child's or adolescent's refusal to talk may be their initial response to parental infidelity. Their silence is often an attempt to punish parents—sometimes both of them: one for being the cheater, the other for not being able to prevent the infidelity.
- It's important to give children time to be by themselves to process what has happened, but also to provide the opportunity to be together, even if the subject of marital infidelity isn't brought up.

- Make time to give individual attention to each child, apart from the other siblings. This one-on-one time may help children to open up and tell you how they're feeling.
- When children finally do speak out about you or your spouse having been unfaithful, allow them to talk without commenting or judging what they have to say. Let them know that their feelings are valid. Be aware that children may become very angry toward the unfaithful parent, the betrayed parent—or both—and that it is counterproductive to react defensively.
- Never criticize your child's feelings. Let them know that there is no such thing as a right or wrong feeling, and no shame in having strong emotions.
- Also let your children know that parents have intense emotional reactions to infidelity as well—and that children should expect such feelings to surface. Let them know that this is a family crisis, and that you will all need to learn how to cope with it and learn from it.
- Don't be reticent about getting help for your child or teen from someone you trust—whether it's a relative, pastor, or psychologist. A family visit to a professional counselor can be extremely helpful in getting kids to open up about how parental infidelity has affected them.

UNBURYING YOUR FEELINGS: ADVICE FOR ADULT CHILDREN OF INFIDELITY WHO "ACT OUT"

If you are an adult child of infidelity, how can you finally come to terms with self-destructive behavior that you may or may not recognize as stemming from a parent's history of unfaithfulness? A

crucial part of confronting your past is to face up to your own feelings as a child of infidelity. If you have buried those feelings, chances
are that the rage, sadness, betrayal, and confusion will spill over into
your relationships without your being aware of it.

If you feel emotionally blocked when you think back to yourself as
a child witnessing the effects of infidelity in your household, consider
how you react now when someone betrays you or abuses your trust.
Does your anger or emotional pain seem exaggerated? Do you tend
to suffer over a betrayal more than other people? These reactions may
tell you that you haven't adequately dealt with your feelings as a child
of infidelity.

Also, your choice in partners may reveal unresolved issues concerning your parent's infidelity. If you consistently choose boyfriends,
girlfriends, or mates who are unfaithful to you, it may be that you are
trying to reenact the betrayal that one parent inflicted upon the other.
It may not be a coincidence that every partner you connect with turns
out to be unfaithful. And if you are the betrayer, it likewise may be no
accident that, as a child of infidelity, you consistently choose partners
with whom you can replay your parents' betrayal drama.

The key to dealing with the infidelity issues from your past is to
take an honest look at your present behavior and think about how it
might be connected to what happened between your parents. What
unacknowledged lessons did you learn from your parent's infidelity?
Was the infidelity drama so painful that you distracted yourself from
feeling its effects by engaging in self-abusive behavior? How did witnessing one parent betray and lie to the other affect your own choice
of a partner and your expectations of that person? Perhaps you had
a sense of wanting to protect yourself from infidelity and thus chose
someone who is a "safe bet" but who you now feel may not be the
right one for you. Or maybe your means of self-protection is to dis-

tance yourself from your partner so that you won't get as hurt should that person betray you. If that's the case, you may eventually realize that your detachment means you're not fully committed to the relationship, which makes it weaker and—ironically—can open it up to the possibility of affairs.

Rather than unconsciously acting out your pain and disillusionment by engaging in such scenarios, wouldn't it be better to start facing your past as a child of infidelity—so that you can develop a stronger, happier relationship with your present partner or one you've yet to meet? One of the most effective ways to do this is to consult with a psychologist who is sensitive to the issue of parental infidelity and to explore with her or him how your current behavior may have been influenced by the betrayal scenario you witnessed as a younger person.

EIGHT

Can I Forgive My Unfaithful Parent?

Seeing my father making efforts to gain back my mother's faith in him made me believe he was sincere in asking for forgiveness. And once I realized that I've been forgiven for all of my sins, how could I not forgive my father for the hurt that he caused?

—*Brenda, thirty-three*

One time my mom did ask for our forgiveness. We were eating dinner, me and my brothers and her, and she said, "I made some mistakes . . ." but I didn't feel like it was very heartfelt. Maybe it was, I don't know. I remember she started crying.

—*Grace, twenty-five*

I'm not sure if I really did forgive my father. I went through
the motions of it, and I thought I did at the time, right before
he died . . . but I feel a lot of frustration because I never really
got to understand why he did it.

—*Jane, fifty-nine*

Forgiving is not condoning. Nor is it an agreement to ignore wrongdoing. Forgiving is about accepting human frailty, even in your own
parents whom you look to as your primary role models. But to come
to that acceptance, as an older child or adult child of infidelity, you
must go through a process of understanding, expressing, and letting
go of your resentments: understanding your family's infidelity crisis
and how you were affected by it, working through and expressing
your feelings about it, and then finally relinquishing your anger and
resentment toward your parent or parents.

In this chapter, we'll hear from adult children of infidelity who
grappled with the issue of forgiveness, some successfully and others
less so. One woman talked about "going through the motions" of forgiving her father but never really feeling she had done so. Another
was influenced by her betrayed mother having forgiven her father,
which inspired her to let go of her own lingering bitterness. Other
adult children still cannot bring themselves to forgive, because the
pain and the anger seem too intense—or they are waiting for their
parent to apologize.

Throughout this chapter we will explore how children of infidelity
can finally come to terms with and accept their parents' flaws and
weaknesses—and move on with their own lives. Like those whose
stories we'll hear, if you are a child of infidelity who wants to forgive
a parent, you will need to confront such difficult questions as these:

Can I accept that someone I love and trusted has done something wrong? Can I accept that my parent failed to live up to his/her professed moral values? Can I accept that my parent unintentionally hurt me, yet still loves me? Can I accept that one parent deeply hurt the other? Can I forgive the parent who cheated even if my betrayed parent cannot? Again, to accept does not mean to excuse; it means recognizing that every human being is imperfect and that even those whom we once held in high esteem can make unwise choices.

The act of forgiveness is highly revered in every religious tradition, and we'll take a look at why forgiving those who have wronged us has always been encouraged by spiritual leaders. Psychologists who study forgiveness encourage it as well, attesting to its emotional and physical benefits, and we'll also explore what they have to say. But first let's hear from Jane, who wanted to forgive her father but faced a persistent obstacle: his unwillingness to discuss his transgressions.

Jane's Story: "I can't forgive my father for insisting his unfaithfulness was none of my business."

Jane is the youngest of three daughters, all of whom were shocked to discover that their father had been cheating on their mother for the last fifteen years of their parents' "basically very happy" twenty-six-year marriage. Jane was nineteen on the day that her father's secret life was exposed.

I was home from college. The phone rang, and I picked it up and it was a man's voice. I jokingly said to my mother, "Oh, it's a man for you, Mom," and I looked out the window, my father was outside, and he had sort of a strange look on his face—almost like he had anticipated this. He came running inside, and my mom was on the phone, and I thought she was going to have a heart attack—she just screamed, "Oh, so that's what it is!" And it turned out that it was my father's lover's husband, saying, "Tell your husband to stay away from my wife." But it was much worse than my father only having that one lover, because that day he told my mom that he had been having affairs with different women for the past fifteen years. And then he packed his suitcases and left.

But before Jane's father left that day, there was much drama in the household. After the phone call from the irate husband, Jane's father told her and her older sister, who was also home for the weekend, to leave him and their mother alone and to go into another room. The lover's husband knocked on the door, and there was shouting and accusations. The man left, Jane's parents talked for a while, but there was no discussion between the daughters and their father, no explanation of what was happening. Just an abrupt ending to a long-standing marriage and a family life that Jane had described as "fairly normal—in fact, my parents never fought, ever." Jane said she felt . . .

. . . like my whole life had come to an end . . . I think what really got me the most was his lying to us for all those years. I felt like he had lied to the whole family. But on that first day he looked at my older sister and me and said, "It's none of your business." That never left me—it was so shocking to me that he would think that we weren't a part of it, when we had been a family.

Jane's father stood firm in his belief that his cheating should be of no concern to his daughters. Jane told me that she tried to talk to him a few days after the life-changing phone call, when he came home to get some of his belongings. She said she had naively believed that he must be in love with the woman whose husband had called, so she asked her father, "Are you in love with her?" He didn't answer her that day (his relationship with the woman ended soon thereafter), nor did he provide Jane with any answers as the years went by.

By letting me know that his cheating was none of my business, it was almost like he was saying, "You're not recognized as a person." About six or seven years later, when I was in my late twenties, I started to write about my feelings about the divorce. I had been having debilitating headaches, and my therapist had encouraged me to write about my parents' breakup, which was still causing me a lot of confusion and sadness. My dad came up to visit me, and I took a walk with him, and I had questions for him relating to the breakup and what I was writing. The first thing he said was, "Don't open that can of worms." And I thought that was a strange expression, because he was the one who created the "can of worms" in the first place.

Jane tried to get some answers from her father by giving him her manuscript about the breakup. She says that since her father had never offered any explanation for why he cheated, she was left to piece together his story with her mother, who had given Jane letters that Jane's father had written to her before they were married. Jane's father was in his twenties then, and his own parents had recently split up— due to his father's extramarital affairs. In the letters, Jane's father told his wife-to-be that he was shocked that his father could do such a thing to his mother—"but then he went ahead and did the same thing," Jane said, "so that was another part of the story that I was trying to make sense of." Jane had incorporated the letters, as well as her feelings and questions and poems, into the manuscript that she asked her father to read. "He read it, but he didn't really say that much," she said, "I didn't think he would. I think it kind of did affect him, but he didn't talk to me about it. It was hard for him to talk about stuff like that."

Jane admits that her mother's idealization of love and marriage made it even more difficult for Jane and her sisters to accept that their father turned out to be so different from the person that they had always assumed he was. Jane's mother claimed she had never known about her husband's affairs until the day of the infamous phone call, so none of the daughters had any clue either. But what seems most difficult for Jane to accept is that her father not only refused to apologize—for lying, for betraying his wife, or for breaking up their marriage—but he also refused to acknowledge that his daughters were profoundly affected by his infidelity. His inability to talk about the behavior that resulted in the breakup of Jane's family made it that much more difficult for Jane to get through the aftermath of her parents' divorce.

My sisters stayed with my mom for about a year after the breakup to kind of take care of her. So they felt that they had sort of gone through some of the transition in a different way than I did, because they were right there with her, whereas mine was more in my head, the trauma of it. . . . I don't know. I think my feelings about my father's affairs and my parents' divorce will always be with me. I was hoping that it wouldn't, that I could outgrow it, but I think I'm still . . . if I were to let go and start crying, I would still feel that pain of him doing that. Of him being such a different person than I thought he was.

Jane is now in her late fifties and continues to feel the sting of her father's betrayal and his inability to provide her with answers as to why it happened. So how has her experience affected her willingness to forgive him? Her father passed away more than fifteen years ago, but in the last years of his life, Jane says that their relationship had improved.

The last five years of his life, when I knew he was dying, I did try to sort of forgive him, and we had a little better relationship. We saw each other a lot more. I told him, right before he died, that I felt better about our relationship. I said that I kind of forgave him for what had happened, although I'm not sure if I actually said it in those words. And I think having given him that manuscript a few years before made me feel that at least I had revealed to him how I felt. Because his not saying anything about it to me or my sisters made me feel that he didn't know how his cheating had affected us.

When I pressed her about whether or not she had forgiven her dad, Jane added this:

I went through the motions of forgiving him, and I thought I did at the time, right before he died, but then I'm not sure if I really did. I feel a lot of frustration, because I feel like I never really got to understand why he did it. I wish that I could know more about his childhood so that I could understand why he became like that, and I'd try to analyze it. I did really feel close to him and loved him, but this shattered a lot of that. I was with him when he died. But I think I still could have tried to find out more before he died about what happened between him and my mom.

It is clear that Jane is still haunted by her unanswered questions as to why her father betrayed her mother, why he became someone so unlike the father she thought she knew, and why he continuously dismissed her need to be acknowledged as an injured party who deserved to know why her family changed overnight. After we concluded our interview, Jane sent me this excerpt from her poem about her parents' breakup:

GHOSTS

They're ghosts to me, my parents

Never together, with me,

Never.

Only to live for illusions not there

There for reality to look in the face

Why can't you see me and see I am real?

I think Jane's story, and her poem, drive home the point that children of infidelity need to be "seen" by their parents as affected parties in the infidelity crisis. Unfortunately, too many parents, like Jane's father, don't understand how severely their children are impacted by parental infidelity. When one parent cheats on the other, the image of the cheating parent and the child's belief in the ideals of love and marriage are shattered. In the aftermath of an infidelity crisis, children need their parents to acknowledge their pain and to offer some sort of explanation. This doesn't mean that parents have to provide details about their sex life or give their children information that is private. But children deserve to be treated respectfully, which means that parents need to recognize that the child has been affected, too.

When Jane's father told her "don't open that can of worms," he was revealing that he didn't want anyone delving into his past behavior, especially his daughters. It is quite likely that he had been unable to sort out for himself why he behaved as he had. Like many cheating parents, he may have felt humiliated by his decisions and wanted to avoid further losing face by keeping the "can of worms" sealed. Unfortunately, when parents who cheat avoid communicating with their children about what took place, they lose even more respect from those children, as many of our interviewees reported.

My sense is that Jane's father may have realized that his daughters had been impacted by his behavior, but perhaps he was unable to face his shame or to express his feelings about why he needed to be with other women. Maybe he wasn't sure why he had that need. Or maybe he couldn't confront the reality that he had fallen into the same pattern as his own father, whose behavior had offended him when he was a young man about to get married to Jane's mother. Whatever the reason for his silence, there is no question that it has deeply affected Jane. Forty years after her parents' breakup, she is still unable to completely let go of her sadness and resentment.

But is it necessary for your parent to apologize or to acknowledge your pain for you to forgive him or her? Can someone like Jane get beyond "going through the motions" and authentically forgive her father? To answer those questions, we're going to delineate the process of forgiving a parent who cheats. At the end of the chapter, if you are a child of infidelity, you'll have an opportunity to explore this process in more depth and to engage in several exercises that will help you initiate it.

THE SIX-STEP PROCESS
OF FORGIVING YOUR PARENT

Forgiving one or both parents for their roles in the infidelity scenario doesn't mean that you ignore or condone what they did. Nor does it mean waiting until they ask you to forgive them, although that does make the process of forgiveness easier. Forgiving your parent means coming to terms with what happened and then allowing yourself to let go of the negative emotions that you've been holding on to.

As a child of infidelity, you can neither deny that your parents' behavior had an impact on your life, nor can you spend a lifetime blaming them for your inability to trust people or to enjoy satisfying relationships. Rather, paving the way to forgiveness involves gaining insight into your parents' behavior and how it affected you; grieving for the ideal parent (or parents) you wish you had had; accepting that your cheating parent, like every human being, is imperfect; and then finding it within yourself to let go of the resentment and anger stemming from your family's infidelity crisis.

As children, we all experience some form of trauma caused by parental misjudgment, neglect, even abuse. Children of infidelity experience a particular type of trauma that can indeed be painful, but it is up to you to take control of your life so that you can make peace with your parent, work through that pain, and then put it behind you. While the memories associated with your parents' relationship may feel immediate and your interpretation of what happened may seem fixed, if you want to open yourself to forgiveness, you will need to be willing to reassess those memories and interpretations. Your cheating parent's infidelity and betrayal—or your betrayed parent's neglect, overdependence, or anger—may have hurt you deeply, but more than likely neither of them intended to cause you pain. Their infidelity drama represented a crisis in their relationship, not an attempt to damage you. While you may feel victimized by what they did or didn't do as parents, blaming them for whatever impact their infidelity crisis has had on you won't help you to heal. Forgiving them will.

What does forgiveness entail? If you are a child of infidelity, the process of forgiving your parent or parents involves six essential steps:

1. Acknowledge how your parents' infidelity crisis affected you.
2. Consider why the infidelity may have happened.

3. Grieve over the loss of the ideal parent (or parents) you wish you had had.

4. Accept that every human being is imperfect, and that your parent(s) is the product of his or her own life history. Accept that even though he/she hurt you and others in your family, your parent probably did the best he/she could given their own personal history.

5. Appreciate the positive aspects of your relationship with your parent(s).

6. Let go of anger and resentment and thereby release yourself from the pain of your past to enjoy a freer, happier existence.

The last step—"letting go of the anger and resentment"—is often the most difficult. As we heard in Jane's story, and as you'll learn from Lucy's, children of infidelity can have great difficulty giving up their resentment toward one or both parents, which is understandable given the serious repercussions that parental infidelity inflicts on children. In Lucy's case, her mother's unfaithfulness had particularly harsh consequences. Nevertheless, Lucy has managed to get through the first two steps in the forgiveness process.

Lucy's Story: "It's hard to forgive my mom, but I understand why she cheated."

When Lucy was about ten years old, her father was diagnosed with a terminal illness, which she now acknowledges "put a lot of strain on my parents' marriage." What she didn't understand as a child was how her mother could start having affairs at the time her father needed her most. Lucy first sensed that something secret was going on when her mother was no longer available to the family either in the mornings or at night.

Up until then, my parents had seemed very happy. But once my father became ill, I think it put a lot of strain on my parents' marriage. It was a hard thing as a kid to understand. I was a little more attuned than my brothers were; I realized that my dad would be dying. What happened was that my mom started having affairs, under the stress of the circumstances. We lived out in the country, and we would all get up and get ourselves ready to go to school. But I kind of noticed that my mom would get up extra early so she wouldn't really have to see any of us in the morning, and then come home extra late at night after we'd all gone to bed. So she was really avoiding all of us.

As she began to relate her family's story, Lucy's attempt to make sense of her mother's affairs was immediately evident. Her explanation that her mom became unfaithful "under the stress of the circumstances" reveals that Lucy, now thirty-eight, has sought to gain insight into the "why" of her parents' infidelity scenario. But a ten-year-old's perceptions about a parent's unfaithfulness can be starkly different than a thirty-eight-year-old's. Lucy recalled having to keep from her father the fact that her mother was taking her and her brother to visit one of her mom's boyfriends. Terribly upset, yet powerless to alter her mother's behavior—or even to express her feelings about it—Lucy's resentment grew.

I remember at the time my dad was really sick. So it was a very difficult thing. I was at that age when I couldn't quite confront my mom about it, but from my perspective I just knew that there was something very wrong with what she was doing, and it was difficult on me, because I felt that she was making me live my life as a lie. Because here she was cheating on my dad, and I kind of recognized what she was doing and that it was not okay—but I couldn't say anything to her about it directly, and I couldn't say anything to my dad. So in a way it made me feel like I was almost cheating on my dad, or I was part of this lie. So that was just extremely difficult.

There were a number of instances when Lucy's distress over her mother's affairs was particularly intense, but she could never let out her feelings. One such incident was when her mother bought her and her brother expensive gifts—a waterbed for Lucy and a minibike for her brother—in return for not telling their father that they were going to visit her mom's boyfriend. Her family didn't have much money, so Lucy realized that her mother's boyfriend must have paid for the gifts. "I looked at the gifts as bribes," she told me. "And I was very unhappy about it, but I felt I had to take the gift. I could have said no to it, but I just didn't know what to do."

After holding her anger in check for another year or so, Lucy says that a turning point came when she could no longer stifle her feelings.

I was sitting on the waterbed, and my mom came into my room and she was kind of upset and she told me that she couldn't handle the situation at our house anymore, and so she was moving out. And I remember, at that moment I stood up to her, and I said, "You know, if you leave this house, I still have to face the things that are happening here. I can't just pick up and leave. My dad's dying—you can't just leave us here. If you leave, you're not my mom anymore, because I don't want you. I don't need you anymore." And then she left.

Lucy's mom moved in with a boyfriend for about six months, then moved back home for a short while, and finally made the decision to take her children and move in with her ex-husband, leaving Lucy's father alone in the final stage of his illness. Lucy told me that the traumatic experience of her mother betraying and then leaving her father has left her with a need to prove her faithfulness in her own relationships—even when a partner is inappropriate or unworthy of her devotion. She revealed that she has stayed in unhealthy relationships too long because she didn't want to be "the kind of person who ever abandoned anybody"—as her mother had abandoned her, her brothers, and her father. Lucy began to cry as she told me that she had spent so much of her childhood in crisis mode that she came to believe she always had to make the best of a bad situation and be on guard to prevent a crisis.

At this point in her life, Lucy says she has little contact with her mother. Still, she has thought about forgiveness.

I was really angry for a long time, but in my early twenties, I really tried to understand, even though I didn't necessarily forgive her; I really wanted to have insight into why those things had happened so I could make sense of it. But it took a long time. I guess in a way it's just a kind of a loyalty thing to my father. It's hard to forgive her, but I understand that it must have been very difficult for her. And I've told her that, too. It was very difficult, but to me I still kind of wish that she hadn't exposed me to that. That if that was going to happen, I would rather she had been discreet about it so that we would not have to know about it. But I think what she was trying to do was to normalize it. I think her father had had affairs, so I think in her mind being unfaithful was an option in life.

Although Lucy hasn't forgiven her mother for having affairs, for compelling Lucy and her brothers to lie to their father, and for abandoning the family when Lucy's father was so ill, it is clear that she feels it is important to try to understand why her mother behaved as she did. Lucy recognizes that her mother's infidelity may be linked to her grandfather's unfaithfulness, that her mother's marriage was stressful due to her dad's illness, and that including the children in visits to her mother's boyfriends was an attempt to "normalize" her mother's affairs. Having gained such insight into her parents' infidelity scenario, and having acknowledged the repercussions in her own relationships, Lucy has taken the preliminary steps in the forgiveness process. Since her mother's treatment of the family was especially hurtful, it may be particularly difficult for Lucy to complete the final step—letting go of resentment.

Lucy is aware of how she continually tries to prove her faithfulness with undeserving partners to distinguish herself from her mother's history of betrayal, and she can use this awareness to motivate herself to change. Finally letting go of her resentment and forgiving her mother will help Lucy move toward healthier relationships. In releasing her anger and pain, Lucy will be able to free herself from her mother's story of betrayal and create her own story. She will no longer need to prove her faithfulness with unworthy partners. Instead, she will feel that she deserves to be happy.

Lucy told me that she didn't want her mom's behavior to ruin her life; she said she didn't want to go through life saying, "Oh, I had such a terrible upbringing, oh, poor me." Instead, she promised herself she would make the rest of her life meaningful. By completing the final stage of forgiveness, Lucy will be able to carry through on that promise.

Wendy's Story: "My mother forgave my father, which helped me to forgive him, too."

Too often the process of forgiveness is made even more challenging when a betrayed parent tries to coerce a child into taking his or her "side," thereby demanding that the child remain angry at the other parent. Children of infidelity often feel pressured to hold a grudge, worrying that they would be disloyal to their betrayed parent were they to forgive the parent who cheated. Unfortunately, when this is the case, a parent-child relationship can be disrupted for years or even lost forever. Wendy's story is happily just the opposite. Her mother's forgiveness of her father enabled Wendy to get beyond her outrage over her father's affair.

Wendy's parents had been high school sweethearts and married shortly after her mother's high school graduation. Over their nineteen-year marriage, they had had typical marital arguments but nothing serious enough for Wendy or her brother to ever suspect that their parents were unhappy with each other. When Wendy was seventeen, her mother discovered that Wendy's father was having an affair with a young woman who was only ten years older than Wendy. Wendy's parents went to several marriage counseling sessions but ultimately made the decision to divorce. According to Wendy, "my father claimed he felt more himself with this other woman than with my mom."

Wendy's mother was crushed by the breakup, as was Wendy: "I was so angry at my father, I couldn't speak to him for months. It made me sick to think of him with this twenty-something girl who he hardly knew—and that he was giving up someone as beautiful and smart and loving as my mother. I wrote him a long letter telling him I had no respect for him at all and that his values sucked, and that he didn't deserve to be married to my mom anyway."

Her father tried to mend his relationship with his daughter over the next few years, but Wendy said she couldn't be around him without constantly "making sarcastic remarks and arguing about whatever." She felt like he was a different man than the one she had grown up with, and she couldn't stop feeling outraged about what he had done. Meanwhile, Wendy's mother went through a painful period herself. She was angry at her husband's betrayal and also very sad over the loss of a marriage to the only man she had ever loved. But after about a year, she began to date and to enjoy her new life.

According to Wendy, her mom has had two serious relationships in the last six years since she and her husband divorced. Neither of the relationships worked out, but Wendy says her mom isn't bitter. In fact, she is still open to love—and has forgiven Wendy's father. Wendy talked about how impressed she is that her mother has been able to forgive her father.

> *My mother has been a role model of forgiveness. She didn't hold on to her anger toward my dad; instead, she worked at figuring out why he had cheated on her. She talked to her close friends about it; she went to therapy. She talks to me about it, too, because she knows I'm still trying to get over this. She told me that he had never really had an opportunity to experiment with different women before they got married—which is what he's doing now. It's not that this doesn't make her sad. It does. In fact, she says she still loves him—and still dreams about him. But she isn't angry at him anymore. She told my dad that she forgave him, and she says that doing it made her feel better.*

Wendy's mother has been able to openly acknowledge and express her anger and sadness, as well as to seek an understanding of why her ex-husband felt the need to have an affair and break off their marriage. Because she was not afraid to face her emotions or to gain insight into her husband's unfaithfulness, Wendy's mother has been able to get to the stage where she can forgive him. When she told Wendy that forgiving her husband made her feel better, she also said, "I did it for myself." Wendy's mom told her that it didn't make sense to forget all the good years she and her husband had together and to remain angry at him forever. She said that by forgiving him she felt freer to treasure the shared history with the man who meant so much to her. Wendy's mother wants to be able to share future family occasions—such as weddings and grandchildren—without the bitter feelings that too often linger in betrayed spouses. Forgiving her husband will allow Wendy's mom to do that.

Witnessing her mother get through this difficult yet enlightening process of forgiveness has inspired Wendy to finally consider forgiving her father as well:

> *Although my mom claims she has never stopped loving my dad, she has moved on. She's had several boyfriends and doesn't hold it against all men that my dad did this to her. She is a thoroughly loving person. Seeing her let go of her anger is making it easier for me to let go of mine. And because she has explained to me some of the reasons why my dad probably did this to her—and to our family—I guess I feel sort of sorry for him. Or at least I have more perspective. I still hate that he did this, but if my mom can forgive my dad, I guess I can, too.*

Wendy's story is a powerful example of how parents continue to be role models even when their children are well into adulthood. Wendy's mother's ability to forgive her unfaithful husband reflected a compassion and wisdom that influenced Wendy in a most constructive and beneficial way.

FORGIVENESS AND RELIGIOUS TEACHING

Forgiveness is highly valued by most religions, and even atheists and agnostics believe that to forgive is to create peace within ourselves. Some religious traditions emphasize the sense of tranquillity that forgiveness bestows on the forgiver; some liken those who can forgive to the most pious or saintly; other faiths refer to God's forgiveness of human sins as the supreme example of why humans must learn to forgive each other.

In Christianity, forgiveness is central to the exemplary life of Jesus. Christians believe that they are obliged to forgive others for their wrongdoing because Christ not only forgives them for their sins but died so that their sins could be forgiven: "Forgive us our trespasses as we forgive those who trespass against us" is part of the Lord's Prayer, one of the most familiar in Christian liturgy. The following passages are also well known to Christians:

> *Peter came to Jesus and asked, "Lord, how many times shall I forgive my brother when he sins against me? Up to seven times?" Jesus answered, "I tell you, not seven times, but seventy times seven."*[12]

> *And when you stand praying, if you hold anything against anyone, forgive him, so that your Father in heaven may forgive you your sins.*[13]

> *Be kind and compassionate to one another, forgiving each other, just as in Christ God forgave you.*[14]

When I spoke with Father Michael Sears of the Servants of the Sacred Jesus, Mary, and Joseph archdiocese of Los Angeles, he had this to say about how Christianity's teachings regarding forgiveness can help children of infidelity to heal:

> *I think a parent's infidelity is a real hard thing to deal with, but Jesus teaches forgiveness for a reason—so that we won't carry the burden of that person's sin on our soul. Forgiving releases it to God. It sets us free to put*

that person's transgressions in God's hands. But it's a hard process. Forgiveness doesn't mean sweeping it under the rug or acting like it never happened; adopting a "get over it" kind of attitude doesn't heal the pain.

In the Christian tradition, we talk about what Jesus taught about forgiveness and how we can apply it to ourselves and know that the grace of the Spirit is going to help us forgive. So a child who wants to forgive a parent is not on their own, in that sense. The great benefit of having faith is in knowing that the Lord is going to provide you with the ability to not only act—in this case, to forgive—but to understand that act. And that's what brings about healing.

Jesus says to forgive "seventy times seven" times, and that it is an act of love to forgive. It's a channel for the child or teen or adult child to begin to love the parent again.

Judaism requires that a wronged individual forgive the wrongdoer if that person sincerely asks for forgiveness and attempts to rectify the wrong:

It is forbidden to be obdurate and not allow yourself to be appeased. On the contrary, one should be easily pacified and find it difficult to become angry. When asked by an offender for forgiveness, one should forgive with a sincere mind and a willing spirit . . . forgiveness is natural to the seed of Israel.[15]

Although a Jew is not required to forgive someone who does not ask for forgiveness, that person may still be forgiven. In such cases, the forgiving person is deemed especially pious:

If one who has been wronged by another does not wish to rebuke or speak to the offender—because the offender is simple or confused—then if he sincerely forgives him, neither bearing him ill-will nor administering a reprimand, he acts according to the standard of the pious. All that the Torah objects to is harboring ill-will.[16]

Rabbi Jocee Hudson of Temple Beth Sholom in Santa Ana, California, explained the process of forgiveness from a Jewish perspective, and why forgiving an unfaithful parent can be difficult yet spiritually beneficial:

> *Jewish tradition requires the offender first to ask forgiveness from the person they wronged and then to ask forgiveness from God. If the wronged person does not grant forgiveness after the initial apology, we are required to ask for forgiveness two more times. This is based on the idea that once a person asks three times and is denied three times, they have fulfilled their obligation. But I think that there is a holiness in this process of asking three times. Sometimes if the first request for forgiveness happens soon after the transgression has occurred, the person isn't ready to forgive yet. He or she may still be feeling the raw emotion—in this case a child whose parent has betrayed his or her trust. The responsibility is on the person who has transgressed to come back and ask again, which allows the person who has been hurt to offer that forgiveness at a later time.*
>
> *For those who have been deeply hurt, but have never been asked to grant forgiveness, it can be empowering to grant it anyway. Granting forgiveness does not mean forgetting past wrongs, and it doesn't necessarily repair damaged relationships or make up for past neglects or abuses. What it does do is offer both the offender and the wronged person a potential path to healing. People I have counseled describe feeling a sense of great relief and peace when they finally grant forgiveness.*
>
> *In addition to Yom Kippur, which is the yearly time of asking forgiveness, Jewish people are supposed to pray for forgiveness for our wrongdoings*

*three times every day. The humility of experiencing that we each have done
wrong to others, have not behaved perfectly, can be a good way to
empathize with someone else's wrongdoing. There's also the teaching that
we're all created in the image of God, and recognizing the divinity of the
other person, no matter how flawed they are, one can come to see them in
a gentler light.*

Moslems are also taught to forgive wrongdoers and to look to God
(Allah) as the role model of forgiveness. The Koran specifically refers
to forgiveness within one's family in the following passage. Followers
are told to forgive spouses and children who may have caused pain by
their wrongdoing or who may cause others to transgress.

*O You who believe! Behold, among your spouses and your children are
enemies unto you: so beware of them! But if you pardon [their faults], and
forbear, and forgive—then, behold, Allah is Forgiving, Merciful.[17]*

A more general admonishment to be forgiving is found in this
passage:

*But withal, if one is patient in adversity and forgives—this, behold, is
indeed something to set one's heart upon.[18]*

Hinduism refers to forgiveness as "the highest virtue" and credits
the continuity of human life to our ability to be forgiving:

*It has been said that the continuation of species is due to man being for-
giving. He, indeed, is a wise and excellent person who has conquered his
wrath and shows forgiveness even when insulted, oppressed, and angered
by a strong person.*

The forgiving acquire honours here, and a state of blessedness hereafter. Those men that ever conquer their wrath by forgiveness obtain the higher regions. Therefore has it been said that forgiveness is the highest virtue.[19]

Buddhist teachings on the importance of forgiveness may be most closely related to certain tenets of modern psychology. Buddhists believe that being a forgiving person is necessary for a state of mental well-being. They teach that resentments have negative repercussions, and they encourage followers to understand the reasons for their ill-will, to calmly release negative thoughts, and to practice loving kindness. Buddhists believe that karma is the sum of all that an individual has done, is currently doing, and will do; thus, feelings of hatred and ill-will leave a lasting effect on our mind karma.

Buddhism stresses freedom from delusion and suffering by meditating and gaining insight into reality. When we fail to forgive, Buddhism advises, we create an ongoing identity based on our pain: "If we haven't forgiven, we keep creating an identity around our pain, and that is what is reborn. That is what suffers."[20] To avoid such suffering and resentment, Buddhism counsels its followers to develop loving kindness (*metta*), compassion (*karuna*), sympathetic joy (*mudita*), and equanimity (*upekkha*).[21]

From the Native American perspective, forgiveness is important because it restores harmony to the individual, the family, and the community. Harmony and balance are deeply valued, as is the respect for "we" over "I." Alberto Sombrero, wellness case manager at the Tucson Indian Center, told me that the Lakota tribe in which he was raised practices a releasing ceremony to facilitate the restoration of harmony and balance. He said that through prayers, songs, talking, and counseling, a hurtful cycle involving parents and children can be broken by making amends and offering forgiveness. If a parent whom one wants to forgive isn't present, he or she can still be forgiven by speaking to the spirit of that person. Members are encouraged to "put everything on the table, talk about it, and find some resolution to whatever the conflict is." What is important is to restore balance and harmony by forgiving.

It is one thing to be aware that your religious tradition encourages, even demands, forgiveness; it is another to put those teachings into practice during the duress of an infidelity crisis. In the following two case histories, adult children of infidelity who initially found it impossible to forgive their unfaithful parent found the path to forgiveness through their deeply held religious beliefs.

Ben's Story: "Forgiving my dad was about changing poison into medicine."

Ben described his father as religious, conservative, and strict. His father had attended church regularly and raised his seven children to respect a moral code that forbid lying, cheating, and sexual promiscuity. When Ben and his siblings found out that their father was having an affair, they completely lost respect for him and resented how he had violated the very values he had hammered into them over the years. Now thirty-nine, Ben was in his early twenties when he discovered his father had a lover. "I was very disappointed in my dad," he told me. "We became distant, and over the years I essentially broke off the relationship with him."

As Ben began to notice that his father was making an effort to heal their relationship, he felt an impetus toward reconciliation with him. But it wasn't until an unusual meeting with a stranger that Ben realized it was his mission to forgive his father.

A friend of a friend contacted me. He said he was developing his skills as a medium and had something he wanted to talk to me about. Even though I was going through a crisis in my life and didn't feel like talking to anybody, something in me made me think, I have to listen to him and I have to believe him.

When we got together, this person told me that in one of his dreams, I had expressed to him that I needed help. I was taken aback, because at that point in my life I really did need help. He told me that one of my missions in life was to reconnect with my father. That was an incredible moment for me because I had never shared how I felt about my father with anybody, and there was no way this person could have known anything about my relationship with my dad. So I told myself, well, if it's part of my mission, I have to do it.

A practicing Buddhist, Ben explained his understanding of his "mission" in terms of his religious beliefs. He told me that Buddhists believe every human being is responsible for his or her actions and that nothing that happens to you is a coincidence. Rather, whatever occurs in your life, good or bad, is a manifestation of your karma, which is the sum of all that you have done, are currently doing, and will do. However, negative karma can be ameliorated through engaging in positive actions. Every positive action that you take in your life helps you advance your spiritual evolution. And, as Ben emphasized to me, "We are all spiritual beings living human experiences, not human beings having spiritual experiences."

As we talked further, Ben spoke more specifically about how his Buddhist beliefs related to his mission to forgive his father:

I realized that my experience of being upset by my father's infidelity was not only part of my karma but my family's karma. I realized that it was easier to blame my dad than to take responsibility for my reaction to what he did. His acts produced disharmony, but blaming him would not resolve the situation. I decided to resolve it from the deepest part of my being, by forgiving, being sensitive to his spiritual evolution, praying and meditating, and having faith that the powerful mantra that I practice would have an impact on my dad's life, as he is part of my world, my environment.

Ben said that what also helped him to forgive his father was his own experience of being tempted by infidelity. Although he is not married, Ben had been involved in several relationships where he was "the other man":

I was myself trapped in infidelity and I realized that it was easy to fall into temptation. True, my experience was different from my dad's; I was single and my actions didn't involve a wife and a family. So the karma that I was damaging was only mine, but in the end it was a learning experience. This helped me to not become judgmental but to concentrate on learning my lessons and to be tolerant in regards to the lessons other people are in the process of learning, including my dad.

I realized that there are some lessons that are not that easy to learn, and they are presented to you several times in life—until you finally learn them, even though those lessons may hurt people that you love.

Becoming "tolerant in regard to the lessons his father was learning" was a key to enabling Ben to forgive his dad. Ben's religious beliefs led him to the realization that his father would eventually learn from the lesson that infidelity offered, just as Ben would learn from his unpleasant experiences with infidelity—both as a child and as "the other man." Ben said that he took advantage of the opportunity to "change poison into medicine" by forgiving his father for hurting him and by considering what he could learn from his experiences as a child of infidelity. I think the wisdom in Ben's story lies in being able to see that our parents' actions revolve around their own life lessons—not simply that Mom or Dad "did this to me." All of our life experiences, especially those that are the most painful, are an opportunity to contemplate what we need to learn. Once Ben was able to see that his father had to grapple with his own life lessons, including the fallout from his affair, Ben realized that he couldn't continue to resent him. Forgiveness was about allowing his father to learn from his transgressions, just as Ben was committed to doing in his own life.

Brenda's Story: "It would be hypocritical of me not to forgive my father since I have been forgiven."

The youngest of three children, Brenda was twenty-seven when she found out that her father had been unfaithful and was planning to move in with his lover. Her outrage was particularly vehement because her father had always taught her and her siblings that "family comes first," and yet, in Brenda's eyes, his behavior had flagrantly ignored that pronouncement. "To me he wasn't choosing family," she said, which is why Brenda told her father that she would no longer stay in touch with him if he continued the affair.

I told him, "I don't understand how when we were growing up you always told us that family comes first, and now a woman has convinced you that she's more important to you than your family." I told him that if this was the decision that he was going to make, he could count on not talking to or seeing me again, because I was so disappointed that he hadn't put his family first. We talked for a while, and I was so nervous because I was thinking the whole time, This is your father—you should show him respect. But I couldn't just sit there and not tell him exactly how I felt, because I knew that what he was doing was wrong.

So he said, "Well, do you want me to go talk to the priest?" and I said, "I don't want you to do anything for me, because it's not me. It's you and it's my mother. You do what you want to do because you want to do it, not because I want you to."

Brenda's parents met with their priest, and her father made the decision to leave his lover and try to work things out with his wife. Still, for nearly a year Brenda's mother continued to be tense and upset, unable to fully trust that her husband loved her and wanted to be with her. Brenda said her mother would often break down crying, still distraught and angry over the events of the previous months. Sometimes she came to Brenda's house for solace:

I would sit with her and ask her, "Why are you still so mad? What's going on?" and then I would help her realize that she was overreacting, because she still had doubts about where my dad was going when he left the house. And that was one of the hardest parts, because growing up my mom had always been the strongest female I ever knew. To see her coming to me for help was very upsetting, but I was there for her.

Although Brenda's father expressed his remorse and was doing his best to prove to his wife that he had recommitted to their marriage, neither Brenda nor her mother had actually forgiven him. Given her Catholic upbringing, Brenda was aware of the need to forgive her father, but she knew it wouldn't be easy.

We grew up Catholic, and we've always been told, "You need to forgive, you need to forgive." It was around Christmastime, and I kept telling my mom, "You need to work on forgiving him. The only person you're hurt-

ing is yourself, because you're still so angry." And she would say, "That's easy for you to say," and I would go, "No, it's not easy for me to say, because I have to forgive my father as well." Anyway, they were having a prayer group at church, and I told my mom, "Let's go, let's go." But she really didn't want to go, and as we pulled up to the church I remember thinking, I feel really bad forcing her to be here when she doesn't want to be here.

But then afterward, when we got back into the car, she thanked me for making her go. I'm not sure exactly what happened during the prayer group, but I remember they were singing about the waters rushing over you and cleansing you, and I was praying and I felt that something had happened. When we got into the car, I was looking at my mom and thinking, Something happened, *but she wasn't saying anything, so I asked, "What happened?" and she said, "I feel like I've forgiven everything that's happened to me." She said [that] she felt that something came over her to grant her the ability to forgive. I asked her if it had anything to do with that song, and she said yes.*

When her mother experienced that powerful sense of forgiveness during the prayer group, Brenda had yet to forgive her father. But in the year or so since her parents' infidelity crisis, she had started going back to church on a regular basis and had begun to consider how she had always been forgiven for her own sins. During a long-term relationship with a man she ultimately broke up with, Brenda had gotten pregnant and had an abortion. She came to believe that the abortion had been a serious mistake, a sin. After her mother's experience during the prayer service, Brenda realized she needed to go to confession. Confessing the abortion and looking into her own past, Brenda discovered the key to forgiving her father:

I realized that I had sinned so much, and every one of my sins had been forgiven. And there's no resentment toward me because of my sins, so how can I continue to resent my father? I was calling my father a hypocrite for not living up to what he said about "family comes first," but then wasn't I being a hypocrite for not forgiving him and being resentful? It's almost as if I was calling myself on having a double standard. I've been forgiven for all of my sins, so how could I not forgive him as well? Once I realized that, it made it easier for me to say, "You know what? I do forgive you."

In essence, what Brenda realized is that both she and her father are human and that every human being makes serious mistakes in life, but when you are sincerely regretful, you deserve forgiveness. After her confession, Brenda felt she had been given the gift of forgiveness from God, and she wanted to offer that gift to her father:

I had not felt forgiven for what I had done until I had actually gone to confession and asked for forgiveness. In that confession, I broke down. The priest was so wonderful, because he was telling me the story of the prodigal son, where the father is waiting for him and they have a huge feast when he comes home. And the priest said that's what it's like every time we sin. God is just waiting for us to come and ask for forgiveness. He's waiting there with open arms to give us that forgiveness. I think that really helped me to realize how much I needed to be forgiving of my father.

Brenda witnessed her father being remorseful and making a serious effort to repair his marriage. Not every child of infidelity experiences that. Still, it is possible to forgive your parent even if he or she doesn't ask for forgiveness or mend the relationship with your betrayed parent. The exercises at the end of the chapter will help you in this process. And who benefits most when you forgive your parent? You do—both mentally and physically.

CAN FORGIVENESS IMPROVE YOUR HEALTH?

Have you ever noticed how your body feels when you are in the heat of anger? Your heart beats faster, your breathing becomes irregular, and your muscles tighten. How about when you're around someone—or just think about someone—whom you still resent for a past wrongdoing? Maybe you don't feel quite as wound up as you do when your anger first flares, but your body is nonetheless in a state of agitation. What all of us know from experience, researchers validate in their studies: when we hold on to anger and resentment, our physical well-being is adversely affected. Conversely, the act of releasing our anger or resentment through forgiveness is shown to "improve cardiovascular function, diminish chronic pain, relieve depression and boost quality of life among the very ill."[22] The Mayo Clinic reported that in one study, subjects who focused on their resentment toward someone had elevated blood pressure, high heart rates, and increased muscle tension. When those same subjects were asked to imagine forgiving the person who was the target of their anger, they reported feeling more relaxed, and the adverse physical changes disappeared.[23]

What about the long-term effects of holding on to anger versus learning to forgive? Psychologist Loren Toussaint and colleagues at Luther University in Decorah, Iowa, were the first to establish a long-term correlation between the tendency to forgive and health. Their findings, published in the *Journal of Adult Development* in 2001, revealed that adults forty-five and older who were able to forgive another person's transgressions were more likely to report good physical and mental health than those who couldn't forgive.[24] And in a 2003 study, Dr. Douglas Russell, a cardiologist with the Veterans Administration, found that after a ten-hour course in forgiveness, the coronary function of patients who had suffered a heart attack improved.[25]

According to some psychologists, the ability to forgive is probably inherent in higher primates and human beings because our survival depends on social cooperation. A forthcoming book by psychologist Michael McCullough of the University of Miami explores the thesis that early humans who were more forgiving, and thus more cooperative, were probably those most likely to survive.[26] McCullough contends that humans were probably designed to be forgiving, but that we can get better at it if we are taught how.

To that end, I invite you to participate in the following forgiveness exercises. Again, the goal for children of infidelity is not to ignore the pain or anger; rather, it is to face and experience whatever emotions you're holding on to, as well as to understand more clearly what went on in your family, grieve over the loss of your ideal parent or parents, and ultimately let go of your resentment so that you are free to live a more satisfying life.

APPROACHING FORGIVENESS: EXERCISES FOR OLDER CHILDREN AND ADULT CHILDREN OF INFIDELITY

Is it possible to forgive a parent who has deeply hurt the other parent, to forgive a mother or father who betrayed your ideal of how a parent should act, or to forgive a betrayed parent for becoming bitter or for putting up with the infidelity? In a word, yes. You can strongly disapprove of how your parents behave and at the same time forgive them for that behavior. You can still honor them for being your parents, and you can still love them for all the ways in which they haven't disappointed you.

I hope that the following journal exercise and guided imagery exercises will help you begin the process of forgiving your parent or parents, because once you are able to do so, you will no longer carry the burden of resentment and will be able to enjoy a more liberated life.

JOURNAL EXERCISE: ACKNOWLEDGING RESENTMENTS TOWARD YOUR PARENT OR PARENTS

1. Write down how you found out about your parent's infidelity—as descriptively as possible. Include not only the details surrounding your discovery that your mother or father was cheating but also how you felt about it at the time.

2. Write down your resentments toward each parent (if you hold resentments against only one parent, write only about that parent), including resentments you had when the infidelity was first discovered and resentments you continue to hold on to. Also include how you have been affected by the way that each of your parents is dealing (or dealt) with the crisis. Take your time writing this, as it will be deeply involving emotionally. You may want to take a week—even a month—to complete the writing. Be aware that writing down your thoughts and feelings may elicit old resentments that you have forgotten about. You may find that you are discovering feelings of anger, hurt, and loss that you didn't realize you had. Don't worry about what feelings are brought up. These are not new emotions; they are feelings you have been holding within yourself. Even when the feelings are painful, let them flow onto the pages of your journal or computer screen. The act of writing them down is healing in and of itself.

3. Once you have completed the journal exercise, you are ready to begin the first guided imagery exercise.

GUIDED IMAGERY EXERCISE NO. 1: GRIEVING OVER THE LOSS OF THE IDEAL PARENT(S)

This exercise is about allowing yourself to feel sadness over the loss of the ideal parent you may have wished for or felt entitled to. Perhaps you thought your parent(s) resembled this ideal before the infidelity scenario, and once his/her unfaithfulness came to light, you became terribly disappointed, angry, and resentful. Working through your feelings will help you let go of your sense of entitlement to an ideal parent and to adapt to the reality of having a parent who is flawed, as we all are.

1. When you have at least thirty minutes to yourself, find a comfortable place where you will not be interrupted. Decide which parent you will be focusing on. It doesn't matter if your parent is deceased, as he/she is still alive within you, and this is an exercise involving your feelings toward him or her.

2. Close your eyes and imagine the ideal parent you always wanted: the parent who is always faithful, and who never lies, cheats, or disappoints you in any way. Perhaps this image is of your actual parent as you perceived him or her when you were younger, before the infidelity crisis in your family.

3. Now tell yourself that, as wonderful as this image is, it is not real, and that for your own health and well-being, you must let it go.

4. Watch that idealized parent disappear—and feel the sadness over the loss of that wonderful, yet unreal parent. Allow yourself to fully acknowledge that the parent you always wanted is gone, because he/she is only an ideal, not a real person. Stay with those feelings of sadness over this important loss.

5. Open your eyes and tell yourself that you have it in you to get beyond the sadness over this loss.

GUIDED IMAGERY EXERCISE NO. 2: RELEASING YOUR RESENTMENTS TOWARD YOUR PARENT(S)

This exercise is about expressing and releasing your feelings to let go of the rage, resentment, and sadness that may be preventing you from having a healthy relationship with your parents and others. Remember that you are not disrespecting or hurting your parents by engaging in this healing process.

1. When you have at least thirty minutes to yourself, find a comfortable place where you will not be interrupted. Decide which parent you will be focusing on. It doesn't matter if your parent is deceased, as he/she is still alive within you, and this is an exercise involving your feelings toward him or her.

2. In your own words, and with an attitude of love, express your decision to rid yourself of the resentment toward your parent for his or her part in your family's infidelity crisis.

3. As if your parent was in the room with you, tell him or her why you still feel resentment for his or her part in the infidelity scenario. (You can do this silently or out loud, whichever feels more comfortable.) Tell your father or mother how his/her behavior has made you feel, whether angry, sad, lost, ashamed, confused, or any other feelings you felt then or feel now. Let your parent know which upsetting feelings you are still holding on to. Tell your parent how his or her part in the infidelity drama affected you when you were growing up, how it affected your ability to trust him/her and others, and how it has affected your relationships. It is okay to scream, cry, or otherwise express your feelings. Give yourself permission to fully release your emotions.

4. To let go of your resentment toward your parent, tell him or her that you are also letting go of your need for an ideal family. You acknowledge that your family was not ideal because it was disrupted by infidelity (and perhaps for other reasons as well). Although your parent or parents did not provide you with the parenting and/or home life that you expected, you now understand that expectations are the idealized notions of what we want, and very few of us receive exactly what we want from our parents. Perhaps your parent was too involved in the infidelity conflict to be fully available to you. Maybe you resented your parent for being a hypocrite—for modeling behavior that strongly conflicts with the values he or she espoused. You may have resented as well that your parent forced you to take care of him/her emotionally or solve his/her conflicts. Your resentment may have stemmed from his/her failure to realize that your ongoing lack of trust, and/or feelings of confusion, shame, self-doubt, or anger were a consequence of the family's infidelity scenario. Tell your parent that you now realize that although all families do not undergo an infidelity crisis, no family is ideal. Every child suffers from parental mistakes. So whatever you expected from your parent that he or she did not provide, you now acknowledge that his/her failings don't mean your parent doesn't love you. Tell your parent that you accept that he or she is flawed, because no parent is without flaws. Let go of your need for the ideal family by expressing to your parent that you accept him or her as the imperfect person he/she is.

5. As you express your feelings to your parent, visualize him or her hearing you, acknowledging your pain, and understanding your feelings. While you perceive your parent hearing you, feel that you are understood and that your father or mother is support-

ing you emotionally. He or she is listening and comforting you—aware of how you are feeling and giving you love in exchange for the honesty you have shown in expressing your feelings. As you imagine yourself receiving the healing love of your parent, feel that love that you always wanted to receive, a love that is not contaminated by the events surrounding the infidelity drama. Accept that healing parental love. You might think of this love as a permanent light of love, a symbol of the love that connects you to your parent. There is an intimate, indestructible relationship between your parent and you—a relationship of love that is independent from any other relationships.

6. When you are finished with this visualization, you can keep the light within yourself and always feel the love connecting you to your parent.

7. If you choose to do this exercise focusing on your other parent, wait at least a few days. Give yourself time to internally heal the relationship with the first parent. Take a week, a month, even longer. Feel the light of love for your parent, independent of whatever your parent may have done. When you are ready, do the same exercise with a focus on the other parent. Again, your intention is to free yourself of any resentment, accept your parent as a flawed human being, and forgive him or her.

AFTER THE FORGIVENESS EXERCISES: COMMUNICATING WITH YOUR PARENTS

Once you let go of your anger and resentment and forgive your parent, you will no longer feel the need to perpetuate the conflict between the two of you or to distance yourself from him/her. You will find yourself better able to communicate with your parent in a mature and open way.

If your parents are still alive, and if they are open to hearing you, you can convey to them what you have learned through these exercises. It is possible that both parents will be willing to listen to you and be open to the possibility of creating a better relationship with you. Even if they aren't open to it, however, you can still be internally connected to your parents through the light of love that you experienced in the visualization exercise. Once you have had that intimate internal conversation in which you express your feelings, receive love from your parent, and return that love, it will be easier for you to connect with your parent in real life and to accept the reality of your current relationship with him or her.

If you do decide to openly express your feelings to your parent or parents about how you were impacted by their infidelity scenario, you will most likely need support from a significant other. An honest talk in which you disclose your feelings may be overwhelming—for you and for them. It is important not to be accusatory. Rather than saying, "You did this, this, and this to me," or "It is because of what you did that I have suffered," tell your father or mother that, "My life was impacted by what happened between you and dad (or you and mom)" and then follow up with a statement such as this: "I realize that we are all human and make mistakes, and therefore I have forgiven you. I want to be free of the resentment I've been holding on to."

Your parent or parents may want to express their own feelings about what happened. If this is so, it is important for you to listen to them and try to understand how they feel. Listening and allowing your parent to express why they made the decisions they made doesn't mean that you need to agree with them. What you're seeking is clarification of their point of view. Understanding their perspective doesn't mean agreeing or taking sides. And listening to their take on the infidelity story doesn't involve arguing. You just need to be an active listener without judgment but with the intention to show your love for your parent by hearing what they have to say.

Again, it is important to have a good friend or spouse, a psychologist, minister, or rabbi when you decide to share with your parent or parents your intention of letting go of your resentments. This third party has to be someone you trust who can listen without being judgmental or critical, someone who can comfort you if you experience upsetting emotions during the meeting with your parent.

Understand that your parents may not be willing to listen to your thoughts and feelings about how their infidelity scenario affected you. They may deny that they hurt you. They may claim that whatever happened between the two of them had nothing to do with you. They may even blame you for not acting differently and thereby avoiding any negative consequences. However, even if your parent is unwilling to accept that their behavior had an adverse impact on you, you can still let go of your resentment through the above exercises. You can still have an internal conversation with your parent during which you express your feelings and they understand you.

Healing from the effects of parental infidelity is not a simple process. But it is also not dependent on having your parent say "I'm sorry." Although it is a parent's responsibility to ask for forgiveness for hurting you, he or she is not always able to do so. And you cannot place your life on hold until a parent realizes that the consequences of parental infidelity can be very painful for a child or an adult child.

To continue to feel victimized is to continue feeling frustrated and resentful. Blaming your parents will not set you free. Even if you are critical of your parent's behavior, you can seek to understand his or her story and how it affected you—and you can choose to forgive. As a child of infidelity, you can acknowledge that you were impacted by your parents' mistakes while also accepting that they did the best they could. In forgiving your parent, you can focus on the love that still exists between you—and you can set yourself free to enjoy your own relationships on your own terms.

APPENDIX

A Word About the Parents Who Cheat Survey:

Our survey is not a scientific study, as there was no control group and our method of acquiring survey respondents did not ensure a sampling that is necessarily representative of the general population. Survey respondents were solicited via the Internet, by invitation through a website, or by receiving an e-mail. Nevertheless, reaching out to potential respondents in this fashion was an efficient way of collecting information from a large number of people whose parents had cheated and who agreed to answer questions concerning their attitudes, values, beliefs, and past behavior pertinent to parental infidelity.

Since our survey is not a scientific one, we do not know how the attitudes, beliefs, and behavior of those children of infidelity who did not respond might differ from those who did respond. Did a majority of nonrespondents fail to respond to our survey because they weren't very affected by their parent's infidelity? And were those who did respond more affected by parental infidelity than those who didn't? We have no way of knowing. It is possible that the people who chose to respond to our survey differ from those who did not respond, thus biasing our findings somewhat.

PARENTS WHO CHEAT SURVEY RESULTS
TOTAL RESPONDENTS: 822

Gender
Female: 84.4%

Male: 15.6%

Age	Total	Female respondents	Male respondents
15–19:	7.8%	6.8%	13.4%
20–25:	15.6%	15.9%	14.2%
26–30:	17.6%	19.0%	9.4%
31–40:	29.9%	29.2%	33.9%
41–50:	15.5%	15.6%	15.0%
51–60:	10.5%	10.6%	10.2%
61–99:	3.1%	2.9%	3.9%

Where do you live?

United States:	87.0%	87.8%	84.1%
Mexico:	1.7%	1.3%	3.5%
Canada:	3.3%	3.1%	3.5%
South America:	0.6%	0.4%	1.8%
Europe:	3.6%	3.6%	3.5%
Other:	3.3%	3.4%	2.7%

Which parent cheated?

Mother:	15.9%	15.1%	20.0%
Father:	73.3%	74.4%	67.2%
Both parents:	14.3%	13.8%	16.8%

Age	Total	Female respondents	Male respondents
How old were you when you found out about your parent(s) cheating?			
5 or younger:	6.4%	6.3%	7.2%
6–10:	22.4%	23.3%	17.6%
11–13:	20.7%	20.1%	24.0%
14–18:	24.3%	24.1%	25.6%
19–25:	15.5%	15.6%	15.2%
25–40:	9.9%	9.6%	10.4%
40 or older:	0.9%	1.0%	0

Did your parents get divorced as a consequence of the infidelity?

Yes:	42.0%	42.5%	40.0%
No:	58.0%	57.5%	60.0%

Were you ashamed or embarrassed to talk about your parent's infidelity with your friends or other people?

Yes:	62.5%	63.1%	59.2%
No:	37.5%	36.9%	40.8%

Did your relationship to the unfaithful parent change?

Yes:	75.1%	76.8%	65.9%
No:	24.9%	23.2%	34.1%

Did your relationship to the betrayed parent change?

Yes:	57.7%	59.6%	47.6%
No:	42.3%	40.4%	52.4%

Were you angry with or hurt by your parent for being unfaithful?

Yes:	88.4%	90.3%	78.5%
No:	11.6%	9.7%	21.5%

	Total	Female respondents	Male respondents

If you were angry with or hurt by your parent for being unfaithful, were you eventually able to forgive him/her?

	Total	Female respondents	Male respondents
Yes:	45.2%	44.4%	50.0%
No:	20.6%	22.1%	11.5%
Cannot answer:	34.3%	33.4%	38.5%

Did you feel betrayed by your parent's infidelity?

Yes:	75.7%	78.0%	63.4%
No:	24.3%	22.0%	36.6%

Was your attitude toward love and relationships affected by your parent's infidelity?

Yes:	80.2%	82.7%	66.9%
No:	19.8%	17.3%	33.1%

Have your own romantic relationships been affected by your parent's infidelity?

Yes:	73.2%	76.1%	57.7%
No:	26.8%	23.9%	42.3%

Do you believe in commitment?

Yes:	89.8%	89.6%	91.0%
No:	10.2%	10.4%	9.0%

Do you believe in monogamy?

Yes:	86.7%	87.0%	84.4%
No:	13.3%	13.0%	15.6%

	Total	Female respondents	Male respondents

Have you ever been unfaithful yourself?

	Total	Female	Male
Yes:	44.1%	43.8%	44.7%
No:	55.9%	56.2%	55.3%

Do you believe that cheating is okay as long as your partner doesn't find out?

	Total	Female	Male
Yes:	4.0%	3.4%	6.5%
No:	96.0%	96.6%	93.5%

Do you believe that people regularly lie?

	Total	Female	Male
Yes:	83.0%	82.5%	85.6%
No:	17.0%	17.5%	14.4%

Do you believe that you should not open yourself emotionally in order to prevent the pain of being betrayed?

	Total	Female	Male
Yes:	41.5%	43.2%	32.0%
No:	58.5%	56.8%	68.0%

Are you concerned about being betrayed by your significant other?

	Total	Female	Male
Yes:	62.5%	65.0%	49.2%
No:	37.5%	35.0%	50.8%

Did your parent's infidelity affect your ability to trust others?

	Total	Female	Male
Yes:	70.5%	72.9%	57.6%
No:	29.5%	27.1%	42.4%

	Total	Female respondents	Male respondents

Do you believe that your ability to relate to your partner would have been different if your parent had not cheated?

Yes:	67.7%	69.7%	56.9%
No:	32.3%	30.3%	43.1%

If your parent's infidelity affected you, please describe how.

(Respondents were invited to write as much as they wanted about their parental infidelity experience.)

RESPONSES TO KEY QUESTIONS BROKEN DOWN BY GENDER OF RESPONDENT AND GENDER OF CHEATING PARENT

MALES WHOSE FATHER CHEATED

Were you angry with or hurt by your parent for being unfaithful?

Yes: 79.0%

No: 21.0%

Did you feel betrayed by your parent's infidelity?

Yes: 65.9%

No: 34.1%

Was your attitude toward love and relationships affected by your parent's infidelity?

Yes: 65.1%

No: 34.9%

Are you concerned about being betrayed by your significant other?

Yes: 45.8%

No: 54.2%

MALES WHOSE MOTHER CHEATED

Were you angry with or hurt by your parent for being unfaithful?

Yes: 80.0%

No: 20.0%

Did you feel betrayed by your parent's infidelity?

Yes: 60.0%

No: 40.0%

Was your attitude toward love and relationships affected by your parent's infidelity?

Yes: 68.0%

No: 32.0%

Are you concerned about being betrayed by your significant other?

Yes: 54.2%

No: 45.8%

FEMALES WHOSE FATHER CHEATED

Were you angry with or hurt by your parent for being unfaithful?

Yes: 91.5%

No: 8.5%

Did you feel betrayed by your parent's infidelity?

Yes: 80.0%

No: 20.0%

Was your attitude toward love and relationships affected by your parent's infidelity?

Yes: 85.1%

No: 14.9%

Are you concerned about being betrayed by your significant other?

Yes: 67.8%

No: 32.2%

FEMALES WHOSE MOTHER CHEATED

Were you angry with or hurt by your parent for being unfaithful?

Yes: 89.3%

No: 10.7%

Did you feel betrayed by your parent's infidelity?

Yes: 76.0%

No: 24.0%

Was your attitude toward love and relationships affected by your parent's infidelity?

Yes: 73.5%

No: 26.5%

Are you concerned about being betrayed by your significant other?

Yes: 53.9%

No: 46.1%

MALE VS FEMALE "YES" RESPONSES WITH SIGNIFICANT DIFFERENCES WHEN MOTHER, FATHER OR BOTH PARENTS CHEATED

	Mother cheated	Father cheated	Both Parents cheated
1. Did your parents get divorced as a consequence of the infidelity?			
Female respondent	43.7%	40.6%	50.5%
Male respondent	60.0%	33.7%	50.0%
2. Were you ashamed or embarrassed to talk about your parent's infidelity with your friends or other people?			
Female	71.2%	63.5%	55.3%
Male	44.0%	63.9%	57.1%
3. Was your attitude toward love and relationships affected by your parent's infidelity?			
Female	73.5%	85.1%	80.9%
Male	68.0%	65.1%	70.0%
4. Have your own romantic relationships been affected by your parent's infidelity?			
Female	61.2%	80.0%	74.5%
Male	54.2%	43.4%	60.0%

	Mother cheated	Father cheated	Both Parents cheated

5. Do you believe that you should not open yourself emotionally in order to prevent the pain of being betrayed?

| Female | 40.4% | 43.5% | 45.2% |
| Male | 16.7% | 27.7% | 52.4% |

6. Are you concerned about being betrayed by your significant other?

| Female | 53.9% | 67.8% | 58.5% |
| Male | 54.2% | 45.8% | 60.0% |

7. Did your parent's infidelity affect your ability to trust others?

| Female | 63.5% | 75.9% | 66.0% |
| Male | 64.0% | 54.2% | 66.7% |

8. Do you believe that your ability to relate to your partner would have been different if your parent had not cheated?

| Female | 65.0% | 72.8% | 55.9% |
| Male | 66.7% | 53.1% | 70.0% |

COMMENTARY

There are a number of survey findings that I believe deserve my commentary, as they point to particularly relevant issues surrounding parental infidelity.

One of the most striking findings is that 86.7 percent of our respondents said they believe in monogamy, and 96 percent said they don't believe that cheating is okay even when their partner doesn't find out—and yet nearly half, 44.1 percent, have been unfaithful themselves. I did not interview every respondent; however, based on the interviews I did conduct, as well as the explanatory section at the end of the survey, most of those who were unfaithful were unfaithful during the first stages of their relationship, after which time they realized that infidelity did not resolve their problems nor did it fulfill their emotional needs.

I believe that being exposed to parental infidelity provokes intense insecurity in children and adult children and thus creates the need to resolve unfinished emotional business by engaging in the same pattern of behavior. Many adult children of infidelity repeat the same behavior as a way to act out, understand, and/or overcome what took place between their parents. From my conversations with those adult children of infidelity who were themselves unfaithful, it is apparent that cheating on their spouse or significant other ultimately convinced them that this was not the right path for them. So, although these particular statistics tend to indicate a contradiction between respondents' attitudes and their behavior, it is my belief that their own unfaithfulness was an attempt to work through their feelings concerning their parents' infidelity.

Another finding that merits comment is the fact that 58 percent of our respondents' parents did not divorce after infidelity was discovered. In my opinion, this means that one or more of the following was likely the case in those families:

- The parents believed that marriage is preferable to divorce.
- The parents were able to understand the dynamics of their relationship and found ways to preserve it.
- The parents accepted infidelity as part of their lives.

Although most experts agree that between 40–50 percent of

marriages end in divorce, studies continue to reveal that a much higher percentage of people are still in favor of marriage. The fact that more than half of our respondents' parents stayed together is also an indicator that people have hopes that even after an incidence of infidelity, things can be worked out.

The interviews I conducted, as well as the explanations at the end of the survey, revealed that some of these parents worked things out and some never did. In the cases where parents were able to work through the aftermath of infidelity, it was much easier for the children to resolve problematic issues, because they learned problem-solving skills from their parents. When parents stayed married but continued fighting and confronting each other in anger, their children's lives became much more difficult.

With regard to parents who divorced, it is interesting to note that more divorces were reported when the mother was the cheater than when the father was the unfaithful spouse, reinforcing a societal attitude that it is a worse offense when a woman is unfaithful than when a man is.

How was the child of infidelity's ability to trust others affected when parents divorced versus when they stayed together? When divorce occurred, 75.4 percent of respondents reported their ability to trust being affected, versus 66.8 percent when parents did not divorce. I believe this discrepancy points to the possibility that when parents stay together despite infidelity in the marriage, children may learn that if parents can still trust each other, then they (the children) can trust in their own relationships.

Additionally, when parents divorced, 73.4 percent of respondents reported that their ability to relate to their partner would have been different if their parent had not cheated; compared to 64 percent when parents did not divorce.

When assessing whether or not respondents were ashamed or

embarrassed to talk about their parents' infidelity with friends or other people, it was surprising to find that they were more ashamed or embarrassed when their parents did not divorce (67.4%) than when their parents did divorce (57%). What I gathered from interviews with and comments from respondents is that it was often difficult for them to understand why their parents were still together after such a betrayal, which accounts for the discrepancy in the above figures.

Another interesting finding was that respondents' relationships with the unfaithful parent changed more when parents divorced (80.1%) than when parents stayed married (71.6%). I believe this was due to greater feelings of betrayal, hurt, and anger toward the cheating parent, whom the child of infidelity tends to blame for the divorce. Our survey results show that there was no significant difference in the relationship with the betrayed parent regardless of whether or not the parents divorced. However, respondents appeared to be somewhat more able to forgive the unfaithful parent when divorce occurred: 50.5 percent were able to forgive when parents divorced versus 41.8 percent who were able to forgive when parents did not divorce. I think these figures reflect that eventually children of infidelity feel the need to repair the relationship with the cheating parent and thus make a decision to forgive. Also, when parents divorce, the infidelity is no longer ongoing; however, infidelity often is ongoing when parents don't divorce, thus making it more difficult for children to forgive the cheating parent.

An additional finding that our survey results revealed is that males seem to be somewhat less affected by their parent's infidelity than females. The percentage of women who reported feeling angry with or hurt by the unfaithful parent was 90.3 percent, compared to 78.5 percent of men.

There was also a notable gender difference in the response to the question "Are you concerned about being betrayed by your significant other?" Females responded "yes" by 65 percent, while only 49.2 percent of males responded "yes." Why is this? I believe that women tend to be more concerned about being betrayed because they are aware of the fact that more men cheat than women; however, their concern about being betrayed is influenced as well by which parent cheated. Females were more likely to be concerned about being betrayed when their father was the cheater (67.8%) than when their mother was the unfaithful parent (53.9%). Similarly, males were more likely to be concerned about being betrayed when their mother was the cheater (54.2%) than when their father was the unfaithful one (45.8%).

As we have seen throughout the book, how a child of infidelity responds to his parent's unfaithfulness depends on the particular circumstances, how the infidelity is dealt with, and the child's relationship with each parent. Certainly culture is also a significant factor. All things considered, however, I believe that children feel more betrayed and hurt when the betrayer is the opposite-sex parent (the mother for men, the father for women). But closeness to the parent, in addition to gender identification, plays a role in how betrayed the child feels.

As for how infidelity affected respondents' ability to trust, there was some discrepancy between males and females depending on which parent cheated. The percentage of females who stated that their ability to trust was affected when their father cheated was 75.9 percent; when both parents cheated, the percentage was 66 percent, and when the mother cheated it was 63.5 percent. Males were more likely to be impacted by a difficulty to trust when both parents cheated (66.7%) or when the mother was the cheater (64.0%) than when the father was the unfaithful one (54.2%).

With regard to the question, "Was your attitude toward love and relationships affected by your parent's infidelity?" 85.1 percent of the females whose father cheated responded "yes" and 73.5 percent of the females whose mother cheated responded "yes." Male responses showed that their attitude toward love and relationships was slightly less affected than females by their parent's infidelity: 65.1 percent of males whose father cheated responded "yes" to their attitude changing, while 68 percent of males whose mother cheated responded "yes." Why the discrepancy between male and female respondents regarding this question? I think women tend to feel more responsible for the relationship and have a greater sense of self-blame when it doesn't work out. Males, on the other hand, are supported by a society that condones male infidelity more than female infidelity. And males are often given the message that it is inappropriate to be overly affected emotionally by relationships. With that said, 65 percent of males admitted that their parents' infidelity had an impact on their romantic relationship, which is higher than I would have expected.

It was not just the attitude toward relationships that changed as a result of parents' infidelity. Respondents also reported that their own romantic relationships have been affected. A higher percentage of females said their relationships were affected when it was the father who was unfaithful (80.0%) and when both parents cheated (74.5%) than when the mother was the cheater (61.2%). These responses can be interpreted to mean that female respondents have a greater tendency to justify their mother's infidelity due to identification with her. The responses from males indicated that their relationships were more affected when both parents cheated (60%) and when the mother did (54.2%) than when the father was the cheater (43.4%).

When respondents were asked if they believed that their ability to relate to their partner would have been different if their parent had not cheated, again females held their cheating fathers responsible more often (72.8%) than their cheating mothers (65%). Seventy percent of males whose mother and father both cheated stated that their ability to relate to their partner would have been different. When it was their mother who had been the cheater, 66.7% of males said their ability to relate to their partner would have been different without infidelity in their family background.

In response to the question "Do you believe that you should not open yourself emotionally in order to prevent the pain of being betrayed?" 40.4 percent of females answered "yes" when their mother was the cheater; 43.5 percent answered "yes" when their father was the cheater, and 45.2 percent answered "yes" when both parents had been unfaithful. Male responses were quite different. When the mother was the cheater, 16.7 percent of males answered "yes" and when the father was the cheater 27.7 percent answered "yes." When both parents cheated, however, males reported being much more reluctant to open themselves emotionally: 52.4 percent. Although I believe that the men who had the courage to answer this survey were more open to discuss what many men cannot, there is significant evidence that males became more reluctant to open themselves emotionally within a relationship when both parents cheated.

And finally, why the discrepancy between the number of males (128) versus females (691) who responded to our survey?[27] I think women tend to be more interested in—and more open about—discussing their family history, relationships, and feelings. My belief is that men generally prefer not to talk about relationship issues, and the subject of parental infidelity may be too painful for many men to confront.

I would like to add that in this survey overall, no significant difference was found between male and female responses to questions that related to being angry or hurt, or feeling betrayed, by a parent's infidelity; both men and women whose parents cheated felt anger, hurt, and betrayal.

I am very grateful to all of the men and women who responded to this survey with honesty and openness, and to those who agreed to be interviewed as well. It is my firm belief that their contributions will help to facilitate the healing process for those who read this book.

NOTES

1 When I refer to "infidelity" in a marriage, I am excluding the concept of "open marriage" (the mutual agreement between both partners that having extramarital sexual relationships is acceptable). While I am not a proponent of open marriage, I assume that parents who practice this lifestyle openly share their values with their children. Whether or not such openness makes extramarital affairs less traumatic for the couple's children is debatable.

2 "A Generation Gap in Values and Behaviors," July 1, 2007, Survey by Pew Research Center.

3 "Up Close and Personal with Sting," *Oprah*, October 28, 2003, www.Oprah.com.

4 The term "parental infidelity" refers to marital infidelity practiced by one or both spouses, who are also parents.

5 MSNBC.com and Dr. Alvin Cooper, www.infidelitycheck.org.

6 www.divorcemag.com and www.infidelitycheck.org.

7 D. Knox, M. E. Zusman, M. Kaluzny, and L. Sturdivant, "Attitudes and Behavior of College Students Toward Infidelity," *College Student Journal* 34, no. 2 (June 2000): 162–64.

8 www.tcm.com.

9 www.opinionjournal.com, February 14, 2007.

10 PBS Online NewsHour, February 5, 1999.

11 *The Dance of Deception*, Harriet Lerner, Ph.D. (New York: HarperPerennial, 1993), 87.

12 Matthew 18:21–22 (New International Version)

13 Mark 11:25 (New International Version)

14 Ephesians 4:32 (New International Version)

15 Mishneh Torah, Teshuvah, 2:10.

16 Mishneh Torah, Book 1, Knowledge: Moral Dispositions and Ethical Conduct, Chapter 6:9.

17 The Koran, 64:14.

18 The Koran, 42:43.

19 The Mahabharata, Vana Parva, Section 27, trans. Sri Kisari Mohan Ganguli; www.hinduism.co.za/forgiven.htm.

20 Abhayagiri Buddhist Monastery, "Preparing for Death" (2006), http:// en wikipedia.org/wiki/Forgiveness.

21 http://en.wikipedia.org/wiki/Forgiveness.

22 "Forgive and be well?" Melissa Healy, *Los Angeles Times*, Section F-1, December 31, 2007.

23 "Learning to Forgive May Improve Well-Being," *Science Daily*, January 4, 2008; adapted from materials provided by Mayo Clinic, via Newswise.

24 "Forgive and be well?" Melissa Healy, *Los Angeles Times*, Section F-6, December 31, 2007.

25 Ibid.

26 "We may be hard-wired to let bygones be bygones," Melissa Healy, *Los Angeles Times*, Section F-6, December 31, 2007.

27 Two respondents failed to state whether they were male or female.

BIBLIOGRAPHY

Ahrons, Constance, Ph.D. *The Good Divorce: Keeping Your Family Together When Your Marriage Comes Apart.* Harper Paperbacks, 1995.

———— *We're Still Family: What Grown Children Have to Say About Their Parents Divorce.* Harper Paperbacks, 2005.

Atkins, Dale V. *I'm Ok, You're My Parents.* Henry Holt & Co., 2004.

Blankenhorn, David. *Fatherless America: Confronting Our Most Urgent Social Problem.* Basic Books, 1994.

Bowlby, John. *A Secure Base: Parent-Child Attachment and Healthy Human Development.* BasicBooks, 1988.

Firman, Julie, and Dorothy Firman. *Daughters & Mothers: Healing the Relationship.* Crossroad Publishing Co., 1997.

Forward, Susan., Ph.D. *Toxic Parents: Overcoming Their Hurtful Legacy and Reclaiming Your Life.* Bantam, 1990.

Fossum, Merle A., and Marilyn J. Mason. *Facing Shame: Families in Recovery.* W. W. Norton & Co., 1986.

Gough, Elissa. *The Teen's Coping Guide to a Parent's Infidelity.* Face Reality, 2002.

Lerner, Harriet, Ph.D. *The Dance of Deception: A Guide to Authenticity & Truth-telling in Women's Relationships.* Harper Perennial, 1993.

Lusterman, Don-David, Ph.D. *Infidelity: A Survival Guide*. New Harbinger Publications, 1998.

Pittman, Frank. *Private Lies: Infidelity and the Betrayal of Intimacy*. Norton Paperback, 1990.

Siegel, Judith P., Ph.D. *What Children Learn from Their Parents' Marriage*. HarperCollins, 2000.

Spring, Janis Abrahms, Ph.D. *After the Affair*. HarperCollins, 1996.

Subotnik, Rona, and Gloria G. Harris, Ph.D. *Surviving Infidelity: Making Decisions, Recovering from the Pain*. Adams Media, 2005.

Wall, Cynthia L. *The Courage to Trust*. New Harbinger Publications, 2004.

Wallerstein, Judith S., and Sandra Blakeslee. *Second Chances: Men, Women and Children a Decade After Divorce*. Mariner Books, 1996.

Wallerstein, Judith S., Julia M. Lewis, and Sandra Blakeslee. *The Unexpected Legacy of Divorce: The 25 Year Landmark Study*. Hyperion, 2001.

Weil, Bonnie Eaker, Ph.D. *Adultery: The Forgivable Sin*. Carol Communications Inc., 1994.

INDEX

A

abandonment, fear of as response to infidelity, 9

Abby (case example), 127–29

abuse, shame and, 69

acceptance, forgiveness and, 200–201, 209

acknowledgement, forgiveness and, 208

acting out
    case example of, 12–13, 16–17, 175–79, 179–84, 184–90, 190–94
    coping with behaviors of, 194–95, 195–97
    of infidelity drama, 173–74
    as response to infidelity, 2, 11–12

addiction, cybersex as, 4

admission of wrongdoing, importance of, 194

adolescence
    development during, 18
    infidelity during, 22–23

Alicia (case example), 29–34

ambivalence
    case example of, 15–16, 16–17
    as response to infidelity, 10

analysis, forgiveness and, 208

Andrea (case example), 125–27

anger
    appropriate venting of, 171
    coping with feelings of, 144–45
    forgiveness and, 209
    impact on health and, 229–30
    parental relationships and, 115–19, 134–35
    as response to infidelity, 2, 92–93, 174

Anthony (case example), 190–94

anxiety, as response to infidelity, 2

assessment, of individual's trustworthiness, 45–46

B

behavioral problems, 115. *See also* acting out

ABOUT THE AUTHOR

Dr. Ana Nogales is a clinical psychologist with years of experience helping clients whose lives have been impacted by parental infidelity. She is the founder of Nogales Psychological Counseling, Inc., and Clinical Director of the nonprofit organization that she founded, Casa de la Familia, established for victims of crime. She practices in Los Angeles and Orange Counties, supervising a clinical program of forty-five bilingual-bicultural mental health professionals.

The author of *Latina Power!* and *Dr. Ana Nogales' Book of Love, Sex, and Relationships*, Dr. Nogales is also a well known media expert who has hosted her own television and radio programs and written an ongoing column for *La Opinion*, the country's #1 Spanish language newspaper, as well as other media outlets.

Dr. Nogales is President of the Association for Latino Mental Health Awareness in Orange County; past president of the Board of the California Women's Commission on Addictions; board member of Women's Transitional Living Center and Las Comadres para las Americas; and a member of three task forces dedicated to eradicating human trafficking: the Los Angeles County Unity Coalition; the Orange County Human Trafficking Task Force; and the Bilateral Safety Corridor Coalition.

Featured at workshops and conferences throughout the United States and Latin America, including the Omega Institute and the Women's Foundation, Dr. Nogales appeared with Nobel Prize Laureate, Rigoberta Menchu Tum at the 2007 Women, Power and Peace Conference.